Debrett's

COOKBOOK
FOR ALL OCCASIONS

Debrett's

COOKBOOK
FOR ALL OCCASIONS

ANTOINETTE SAVILL

WITH HELPFUL HINTS ON WINE
BY GRAHAM GARDNER

DEBRETT'S PEERAGE LIMITED
LONDON · NEW YORK · TORONTO · SYDNEY

ISBN 0 905649 72 9

First published in 1984 by
Debrett's Peerage Limited,
73-77 Britannia Road,
London SW6 2JR

Distributed by J M Dent & Sons (Distribution) Ltd.,
Dunhams Lane, Letchworth, Herts., SG6 1LF

Typeset by Holywell Press Ltd., Oxford
Printed in Great Britain at the Pitman Press, Bath

CONTENTS

An Informal Affair

PREFACE

I have had such fun writing this recipe book, and hope you have as much fun preparing the food and choosing the wines as I did.

There are a selection of complete menus to help you plan your dinner and lunch parties, and a few very funny party games to play afterwards.

I have put together some of the trusted and well-tried recipes which I have used over the last seven years of professional cooking.

There are some quick and easy ones and a few more difficult ones for those of you who are a bit more ambitious or have a little more time.

ACKNOWLEDGEMENTS

I would like to thank Sarah Mackesy for suggesting I take this book to Debrett and helping to bribe them to publish it!

I would also like to thank Graham Gardner of Buckingham Wine Merchants, who has spent so much time choosing the wide range of wines to compliment my food; A. A. King of Parsons Green who have always provided me with delicious fish; my sister Nicky for doing the cartoons, and Joanna Morgan-Grenville for typing it out; my mother for trying endless recipes at her dinner parties last year, and lastly Charles Cassels for his supply of funny games.

In the soup

Cream of Lentil and Bacon Soup

Serves six

Not as countrified as you may think, and very comforting in the winter when you come back from a cold and wet morning shooting.

> 8 oz red lentils
> 1 large onion chopped
> 4 oz smoked streaky bacon
> 1 pint chicken stock
> ¼ pint single cream
> ½ pint milk
> 2 oz butter
> salt, pepper, nutmeg

Sauté the finely chopped onion and the bacon for a few minutes in the butter, season, and add the chicken stock. Boil for 5 minutes and add more milk if the lentils absorb too much liquid. Cook for at least 40 minutes to obtain a smooth cream consistancy. Purée the soup in an electric blender and add the cream. Finally adjust the seasoning with a pinch of grated nutmeg. Delicious with fresh warmed brown rolls.

Wine: I suggest a light madeira for outside or drink whatever will go with the next course.

Hot Watercress and Lettuce Soup

Serves six

This is an ideal way of using up overgrown lettuces in the garden or those not quite crisp enough to merit a salad!

> One lettuce
> 4oz watercress leaves
> 1 small onion
> 2oz butter
> 1 pint chicken stock
> salt, black pepper and nutmeg
> 1 pint milk
> 1 egg yolk
> 5 fluid oz cream

Sauté the onion in the butter, wash the lettuce leaves and pick over the watercress, discarding all the thick stalks. Add them to the onion and cook over a very low heat for 2 – 3 minutes. Pour over the stock, season well and boil for 5 minutes. Add the milk and then simmer slowly for 25 minutes. Remove from the heat and when cool enough, liquidize the soup in a blender, then reheat gently for 10 minutes. Just before serving, add the egg yolk mixed with the cream and simmer until it thickens. Do not boil or it will curdle. Serve hot with crispy bread croutons.

Wine: Muscadet A.C. – A good-value and very popular dry white wine from the Loire valley. Known by some as the smile of France.

Iced Cream of Fennel Soup

Serves six

This is a very refreshing soup for summer dinner parties and lunch parties and is equally delicious hot.

    12 oz (approx 2 heads) of fennel, finely chopped
    1 onion finely chopped
    4 oz butter
    squeeze of lemon juice
    ¼ pint single cream
    1 pint creamy milk
    1 pint chicken stock
    freshly ground black pepper
    2 tablespoons flour

Clean the fennel and chop finely, keeping any of the greenery left on top for decoration. Chop the onion and sauté the two in a saucepan in the butter. Cook for 10 minutes and then stir in 2 tablespoons of flour. Pour over the stock and season. After 5 minutes add the milk and simmer for a further 15 minutes. Cool and liquidize in a blender. Stir in the cream and lemon juice.

Serve in very cold bowls decorated with a little piece of fennel greenery, or failing that, a tiny sprig of parsley.

Iced Spinach and Mint Soup

Serves six

The mint makes this a very refreshing summer soup, so please use fresh mint if you can.

> 1 lb frozen or fresh spinach
> 1 small onion, finely chopped
> 2 oz butter
> salt, black pepper and a little nutmeg
> 1 pint chicken stock
> 1 pint milk
> ¼ pint cream
> 1 handful mint leaves (Reserve 6 mint leaves for decoration)

Sauté the onion in the butter for 3 minutes without colouring it. Add the spinach and continue cooking for a further 3 minutes. Season well and pour over the stock and half the quantity of mint leaves.

Cool for 20 minutes then remove pan from heat. When it is cool enough, liquidize it in the blender with the rest of the mint leaves. Add the milk and cream and return to pan. Simmer for 10 minutes. Set aside to cool.

Chill in fridge. Decorate with mint leaves.

Wine: I suggest a bottle of Perrier-Jouët champagne as an aperitif and save a drop or two to drink with the soup.

Cream of Carrot and Ginger Soup

Serves six

Fresh ginger makes this soup, but failing that, use ground ginger.

> 2 lb carrots, washed, peeled and sliced
> 1 large spanish onion
> 4 oz butter
> 2 teaspoons grated root of fresh ginger
> or 1 tablespoon of ground ginger
> 2 pints chicken stock
> 5 fluid oz cream
> fresh parsley to decorate
> fried croutons of bread
> salt and pepper and nutmeg

Put the sliced vegetables in a saucepan and sauté for 5 minutes in the butter. Add the ginger, stock and seasoning and cook for a further 15 minutes. Cool and purée in a blender. Stir in the cream and keep warm until needed or serve very cold in the summer. Decorate with the parsley and croutons.

Wine: In Bordeaux in March I was offered a young Sauterne as an aperitif – but do not use a Cru Classé.

Cream of Mushroom and Coriander Soup

Serves six

With the touch of coriander, this soup becomes rich, creamy and aromatic – a lovely winter soup.

> ½ lb flat mushrooms, finely chopped
> and any leftover stalks or peelings
> 3 oz butter or margarine
> 1 oz flour
> salt, fresh black pepper, nutmeg
> 3 teaspoons coriander powder
> 8 oz single cream
> 1½ pints chicken stock

Sauté the mushrooms in the butter for a few minutes. Beat in the flour and pour in the stock gradually. Season and leave to simmer for 20 minutes. Put in a liquidizer and return to pan. Pour in the cream and reheat.

Serve with warm bread rolls and butter.

The Perfect Hot Starter

Fresh Fennel
with Hollandaise Sauce

Serves four

Select really crisp and fresh looking fennel. Give each person one small bulb or half a large one. Trim away any discoloured or coarse fibres and scrub clean in cold water.

Boil for 20 minutes in salted water with a glass of white wine added after 10 minutes. When they are tender drain carefully. Meanwhile make the Hollandaise Sauce, recipe on page 123.

Place a piece of fennel on each person's plate and pour the sauce over it.

Wine: Muscat d'Alsace – a spicy wine to set off the flavour of fennel.

Blue Cheese Pancakes

Serves four or eight

These delicious pancakes freeze very well and are a lovely winter starter.

8-10 thin pancakes (refer to page 126) – ½ pint pancake mixture
2 × 4 oz packets Danish Blue Cheese, crumbled
2 oz plain flour
1 glass dry white wine
¼ pint milk
¼ pint single cream
salt and freshly ground pepper
parmesan cheese and butter for browning
1 oz butter

Set oven at 400°F (Mark 6). To make the filling, melt the butter in a saucepan and beat in the flour, slowly add the wine, cheese, milk and cream. Season according to taste. Leave to cool slightly. Fill half of each pancake with the mixture and fold over twice until you have a triangle. Arrange them on an ovenproof dish and sprinkle grated parmesan and dot with butter. Bake until golden and bubbling – about 15 minutes.

Smoked Ham and Asparagus Pancakes with Hollandaise Sauce

Serves six

A very special summer starter, ideal if you have plenty of asparagus in the garden.

> ½ pint French pancake batter (page 126)
> 6 slices of smoked ham
> 18 sticks fresh asparagus
> or 1 8-9 oz can green tipped asparagus spears
> For the Hollandaise sauce or quick Hollandaise sauce (page 123)
> 8 oz butter
> 2½ fluid oz wine vingegar
> 2 egg yolks
> 1 teaspoon whole black pepper corns
> 1 bayleaf

Set oven at 350°F (Mark 4). Make the pancake batter and leave it for 30 minutes. Wash and trim the asparagus and poach until soft in a frying pan of water. Drain ready for use.

Now make six large pancakes, and keep them warm in a clean dish cloth. Lay one piece of ham on each pancake and then place 3 sticks of asparagus on the ham. Fold the pancake up and lay in a greased oven-proof dish. Dot with a little butter and put in the oven for 10 minutes to warm through.

Meanwhile, make the Hollandaise Sauce by placing the vinegar, bayleaf, peppercorns into a small saucepan and reduce to half. Add half a desert spoon of water. Strain into a small bain-marie. Return to a low heat and beat in the egg yolks, thicken slightly and slowly add the melted butter, whisking vigourously. Keep aside for the moment. Alternatively, make the quick Hollandaise sauce.

As soon as the pancakes are warmed through, lay one on each plate and pour over the sauce.

Wine: Mâcon-Lugny les Genièvres – a good but inexpensive white burgundy – the authoress loved it.

Swiss Cheese and Spinach Quiche

Serves six

A very simple quiche that needs to be served piping hot. An easy lunch or supper dish too.

> 1 packet frozen shortcrust pastry or savoury shortcrust pastry (page 124)
> 2 oz butter
> 1 oz flour
> 2 oz grated cheddar cheese
> 4 oz Gruyere, grated
> 4 oz Emmenthal grated
> 5 fluid oz single cream
> 1 glass dry white wine
> 1 very small clove garlic, crushed
> 2 egg yolks
> 1 lb cooked, drained and seasoned spinach leaves
> 1 oz butter and grated Gruyere for browning

Set oven at 350°F (Mark 4). First, make the pastry and line the 8 – 9″ flan ring or quiche dish. Bake the pastry blind until very pale brown. Prepare the filling by melting butter and adding the flour. Cook thoroughly, slowly incorporating the wine, then the Emmenthal and Gruyere, garlic and cream. When this is bubbling, remove from heat and beat in two egg yolks. Cover the bottom of the pastry case with grated cheddar cheese. Then the spinach leaves and finally pour over the cheese sauce. Dot the sauce with butter and Gruyere and brown in the oven for 15 minutes.

Wine: Alsace Sylvaner – probably the best value wine from North-East France. Light, crisp and dry.

A Little Mushroom Tartlet

Little Mushroom Tartlets

Serves six

An excellent starter or savoury made as individual tartlets.

For 12 tartlets

8 oz savoury shortcrust pastry (page 124)

Filling
½ pint Béchamel with 2 tablespoons sherry
¾ lb mushrooms, finely sliced
2 oz butter
A squeeze of lemon juice
Grated Parmesan

Set oven at 400°F (Mark 6). First make the pastry and set aside to chill. Then make the Béchamel sauce, adding the 2 tablespoons sherry and keep warm whilst you sauté the mushrooms in a frying pan in the 2 oz butter. After 2 or 3 minutes add a few drops of lemon juice. Incorporate the mushrooms into the sauce. Now roll out the pastry into ¼" thickness and stamp 12 circles with a pastry cutter. Bake these blind in a baking tray for 12 – 15 minutes until pale brown. Leave to cool on a rack. When ready to serve, fill each tartlet with the mushroom filling and sprinkle with Parmesan. Heat through in the oven for 10 – 12 minutes.

Wine: Beaujolais Blanc makes an interesting change – and won't smother the delicacy of the mushrooms.

Chicken Liver and Mushroom Vol-au-vents

Serves six

You can start this half an hour before dinner, so it's ideal if you are in a hurry. If you make this as a savoury then I suggest that you cook the vol-au-vents and leave to one side ready for use and that you make the filling and leave it in a saucepan ready to heat up at the last moment.

1 packet frozen vol-au-vents (12 in all)
1 beaten egg
2 oz butter
8 oz chicken livers, finely diced
8 oz mushrooms, finely sliced
½ wine glass medium sweet sherry
salt, black pepper, grated nutmeg
5 fluid oz thick cream
1 tablespoon cornflour in a little water
parsley to garnish

Set oven at 400°F (Mark 6). Brush the frozen vol-au-vents with the beaten egg and bake them as instructed. Meanwhile make the filling. Sauté the livers and mushrooms for a few minutes in the foaming butter. Pour over the sherry and simmer for a few minutes. Season well and stir in the cornflour mixture until the sauce is thick. Stir in the cream and mix well.

When the vol-au-vents are ready, remove the lids and spoon the mixture into the vol-au-vents and garnish with parsley.

Wine: A light dry white wine. Valclair House White has a continuity of quality, not usually found at around £2 per bottle.

Hot Avocado in Puff Pastry

Serves six

Here is another excuse for using my favourite fruit, avocado. It is an unusual recipe and always creates great interest when presented at dinner.

> 3 ripe avocados, peeled and stone removed
> 1 tablespoon lemon juice
> 4 oz butter, melted
> salt and pepper
> 1 teaspoon Worcester sauce (to taste)
> few drops tabasco
> pinch of Cayenne
> 1¼ lb puff pastry
> 1 beaten egg

Blend all the ingredients except the puff pastry and beaten egg in an electric blender. Roll the pastry into a rectangle. Fill with the avocado purée and fold over. Seal the edges with the beaten egg, knock the edges up with a knife and decorate with the spare bits of pastry and score a diamond pattern over the top. Make a small hole in the middle to allow air to escape.

Place in the oven at 425°F for 20 minutes until pastry is well risen and golden brown. Serve in slices straight away.

Wine: Mâcon Lugny Les Genièvres – a very good standard white Burgundy from Louis Latour.

It's about time you learned to do a Cold Starter!

Blue Cheese Mousse

Serves four

This is a very light mousse best served in ramekins, sprinkled with Cayenne and served with very thin toast.

> 2 oz Stilton cheese
> 1 tablespoon sour cream
> 2 eggs
> 2 tablespoons double cream
> salt and pepper, dash tabasco
> ¼ oz gelatine
> Cayenne

Dissolve the gelatine in a little water and cool. Separate the eggs, whisk the yolks until yellow and creamy. Add salt and pepper stir in the gelatine and tabasco and blend Stilton and sour cream until smooth. Whip the double cream and whisk the egg whites until stiff. Fold the cream into the cheese mixture and lastly the egg whites. Set in the fridge for an hour or so. Sprinkle with Cayenne.

Ascot Egg Mousse, Darling?

Ascot Egg Mousse

Serves eight

This mousse has survived the liveliest of picnics at Ascot and providing you keep it in the shade won't do anything ghastly, like melt before your eyes!

> 10 eggs, hard boiled
> ½ pint mayonnaise
> ½ oz gelatine dissolved in a little water
> few drops tabasco
> 4 teaspoons Worcester sauce
> 1 teaspoon anchovy essence
> Cayenne or Paprika
> ½ pint whipped cream
> 1 egg white, stiffly whipped
> salt and pepper
> 6 – 7″ diameter soufflé dish

First, dissolve the gelatine and cool. Then chop the eggs finely and mix with the mayonnaise in a bowl. Season and add a few drops tabasco, anchovy essence, Worcester sauce. Fold in the gelatine and when quite cold fold in the cream followed by the egg white.

Pour into a soufflé dish and sprinkle a tiny bit of Cayenne or Paprika. Alternatively finely slice some cucumber to decorate the top of the mousse.

Wine: Vin de Pays Charentais '82 or Fruits de Mer as a drier alternative.

Avocado and Watercress Mousse

Serves six – eight

I suggest that you buy your avocados well in advance and keep them in a warm place to ripen unless you are very lucky and know where you can find ripe ones at a moment's notice!

2 large bunches watercress, leaves only
3 avocados
½ oz gelatine, dissolved in ¼ pint boiling water
salt and freshly ground black pepper to taste
1 tablespoon Worcester sauce
¼ pint mayonnaise
¼ pint double cream (lightly whipped)
few drops tabasco
1½ pint ring mould
1 egg white, stiffly whipped

Oil the ring mould. Prepare the gelatine. Peel, quarter and remove stones from avocados. Crush with a fork or purée in a blender with the watercress. Add gelatine, seasoning, Worcester sauce, and tabasco. When the mixture is cold, fold in the mayonnaise and cream, followed by the egg white. Leave in a cool place to set.

Turn out mousse by dipping for a few seconds in hot water onto the serving dish and decorate with watercress in the centre of the ring.

Wine: Vin de Pays Charentais – an interesting wine, coming from the Cognac district. Excellent value for money. Dry and fruity. This will go with almost anything that needs white wine. Also fit for those horrendous family drinks parties which span four generations.

Spicy Chicken Liver Pâté

Serves eight

Ideal for point-to-point lunches and picnics. This makes a quick and easy change from the usual versions. The pâté freezes very well and will keep in the fridge for 3 – 4 days.

        8 oz chicken livers
        ¼ lb butter
        1 medium onion, finely chopped
        1 clove garlic, crushed
        3 tablespoons sherry
        pinch Cayenne
        1 teaspoon ginger
        1 teaspoon mixed spice
        ½ teaspoon grated nutmeg
        salt and freshly ground black pepper
        2 oz butter for clarifying

Trim any discoloured parts from the chicken livers. Melt half the butter in a large frying pan and gently cook the onions in it until they are soft and transparent. Add the garlic, spices, seasoning and the chicken livers. Cook them gently, stirring occasionally for about 10 minutes until they are evenly browned. Liquidize the mixture in a blender with the rest of the butter when it is cold. Transfer into a suitable serving dish and chill before serving with toast.

If you would like to keep the pâté for a few days, or wish to freeze it, seal the pâté with 2 oz clarified butter.

Wine: Muscat d'Alsace – the spicyness of this dry white is unique. Fruits de Mer – a drier version of Vin de Pays Charentais.

Tomatoes stuffed with Ham and Cheese and Olives

Serves six

Delicious for a summer buffet or starter or with a salad lunch – keep them very cold, they will keep in the fridge all day if you want to prepare them in the morning.

1 packet black olives
6 large tomatoes (preferably the mediterranean kind)
4 thin slices smoked ham, finely chopped
¼ lb cottage cheese
½ lb low fat cream cheese
salt and freshly ground black pepper
Paprika
To serve: lettuce leaves or watercress

Clean tomatoes and pat dry. Cut off lids, and scoop out most of the flesh, taking care not to break the shells. Mix the cheeses, ham and seasoning together and remove the stones from the olives before adding them to the mixture. Pile it all back into the empty shells.

Save six of the largest olives and place one on each tomato. Serve on a dish of lettuce or watercress.

Wine: Chianti or Bardolino – these light Italian reds are perfect for that three hour alfresco lunch.

Courgette and Egg Salad

Serves four

1 lb courgettes
2 hard boiled eggs
½ pint French dressing (page 125)
handful of fresh parsley, finely chopped
fresh French bread and butter

Top and tail courgettes and slice finely. Boil them in salted water until just tender but still slightly crispy. Rinse in cold water and drain. Transfer them into a salad bowl and sprinkle the finely chopped eggs over the top. Pour over the french dressing and toss the salad. Sprinkle parsley over the top.

Chill in the fridge for a few hours and serve with fresh French bread.

Wine: Bordeaux Dry Sauvignon. Greatly under-rated, this represents good quality wine from a very sound grape – crisp but with plenty of fruit.

Iced Baby Onions in Tomato Sauce

Serves eight

For this recipe you can be very clever and rush off to your nearest supermarket and buy a large packet of frozen baby onions; this will save you a great deal of time and lots of tears.

2 lb baby onions or
2 lb packet of frozen baby onions
2 tins chopped tomatoes
1 oz tomato purée
1 teaspoon mixed herbs
1 bayleaf
salt and freshly ground black pepper
2 cloves garlic, crushed
2 glasses red wine
8 tablespoons olive oil
2 tablespoons wine vinegar
1 tablespoon sugar

Peel the fresh onions and wash them in cold water, or thaw the frozen onions slightly. Sauté them in the olive oil for a couple of minutes and stir in the tomatoes and the purée and then add the remaining ingredients. Cook slowly for 40 minutes stirring gently from time to time. Transfer to a serving dish and cool.

Garnish with parsley and serve with warm French bread.

Wine: a light red Italian wine always goes well with tomato – either a Valpolicella or Chianti.

Avocado filled with Crab and Almonds

Serves four

The different textures of crunchy apples, toasted almonds with the fine flavour of crab combine to make an unusual and special starter.

2 ripe avocados
2 tablespoons mayonnaise
2 drops tabasco
½ teaspoon anchovy essence
½ teaspoon lemon juice
2 tablespoons almonds, toasted
3 oz crab meat
½ apple cut into tiny bits
salt and pepper
¼ pint whipped double cream

Halve the avocados, remove the stones and sprinkle a little lemon juice over them to stop them from going brown. Mix the mayonnaise, whipped cream, crab meat, toast almonds, anchovy essence, tabasco and lemon juice. Season with salt and pepper. Fold the apple carefully into the mixture and spoon into the avocados. Serve with devilled water biscuits (see page 34).

Wine: Decugnano dei Barbi Orvieto Classico (Secco) or Soave.

Devilled Water Biscuits

Simply delicious to serve with savoury mousses and all sorts of hors d'oeuvres.

> Small water biscuits
> Melted butter
> Cayenne pepper

Set oven at 400°F (Mark 6). Brush the biscuits with the melted butter, sprinkle very lightly with the pepper. Lay on a baking tray and heat until piping hot – about 4 – 5 minutes.

Scallop and Bacon Vol-au-vents

Serves six

A special treat for all scallop-lovers and would definitely impress everybody.

            1 packet of 12 frozen or bought vol-au-vents
            ½lb large fresh or frozen scallops, diced into ½″ cubes
            6 rashers smoked back bacon cut into thin strips
            1 large glass dry white wine
            5 fluid oz thick cream
            4 oz unsalted butter
            2 oz flour
            juice of half a lemon
            season according to taste, with salt and black pepper
            parsley to garnish
            1 beaten egg
            2 egg yolks

Set oven at 350°F (Mark 4). Brush the vol-au-vent cases with a beaten egg and bake in the oven for 20 minutes. Remove from oven and cut out the tops. Set aside. Melt the butter in a saucepan and sauté the bacon for a few minutes, stir in the flour, pour in the wine and lemon juice and cook for a further few minutes, followed by the scallops and cream. Pour this mixture into each vol-au-vent case and serve immediately, garnished with the parsley tops and parsley.

Wine: I suggest a light white wine such as a northern Italian or a dry Loire wine.

Smoked Haddock Ramekins

Serves six

This can be made in individual ramekins as a starter or in a large oven-proof dish as a main course. Try and buy your fish from a fishmonger who smokes his own – the difference is fantastic.

> 1 lb smoked haddock fillets
> 3 hardboiled eggs, peeled and thinly sliced
> 1 lb cooked, drained and seasoned spinach
> 6 tablespoons browned breadcrumbs (fry in butter until golden, drain on some absorbant paper)
> 2 oz flour
> 4 oz butter
> ¼ pint milk
> ¼ pint cream
> 1 bay leaf
> 6 peppercorns

Set oven at 400°F (Mark 6). Poach haddock fillets in the milk with the bayleaf and peppercorns for 15 minutes. Flake into a bowl, remove all the bones and set aside. Sieve the milk and make a Béchamel sauce with the butter and flour and season according to taste. Fold in the fish and cream.

In each ramekin put first the spinach and then a few slices of egg and then the fish mixture and cover with breadcrumbs. Heat through for 10 minutes until bubbling.

Wine: Alsace Riesling or Corvo Bianco; 2 very different white wines, but both have a marvellous amount of body and fruit for the price.

Crab and Asparagus Tart

Serves six

This is a delicious hot starter or savoury and equally suitable for a lunch or a supper dish. The crab freezes well; let it thaw completely and reheat until gold and bubbling on top.

13 oz shortcrust pastry – defrosted if frozen
12 oz crab meat (½ dark and ½ white meat)
¼ pint thick Béchamel sauce
¼ pint thick cream
2 tablespoons medium dry sherry
12 oz can asparagus or 12 sticks of fresh asparagus
2 egg yolks
salt and pepper
Handful grated Gruyere or similar hard cheese
Use a 8-9″ diameter flan ring

Set oven at 350°F (Mark 4). Line the tin with the pastry and bake blind until pale and crispy brown. Meanwhile make the Béchamel sauce by melting the butter in a saucepan and adding the flour; when it is bubbling pour in the milk and then the cream and the sherry, season it and stir in the crab carefully. Remove from the heat and stir in the egg yolks combined with a little leftover of cream.

Fill the pastry case with this mixture and decorate with the asparagus spears. Sprinkle with a little bit of grated hard cheese. Bake it in the oven for a further 20 minutes until bubbling and golden on top.

Wine: Muscadet – or go one better, crab and asparagus sauce deserves it! Try a Chablis A.C. Premier Cru.

Devilled Crab and Banana Pancakes

Serves eight

The bananas make this dish rather unusual, and it also makes a delicious main course with a crisp summer salad.

16 small or 8 large pancakes
1½ lb mixed crab meat
1 tablespoon grated Parmesan
1 teaspoon anchovy essence
1 teaspoon English mustard
2 tablespoons sherry
pinch Cayenne pepper
2 teaspoons Worcester sauce
1 oz butter, diced

salt and pepper to taste
extra milk and butter
¼ pint milk
¼ pint single cream
4 bananas
juice of lemon
4 oz butter
2 oz flour

Set oven at 400°F (Mark 6). Melt 4 oz butter in a saucepan, beat in the flour gradually, adding the milk until you have a roux. Add the Parmesan, anchovy essence, mustard, Cayenne, Worcester sauce and cream. Lastly, fold in the crab meat and cook gently for 5 minutes. Meanwhile, peel each banana and cut into ½ lengthwise, fry quickly in hot butter and sprinkle with lemon juice.

Fill the pancakes with the crab mixture and fold over tightly, lay in a buttered oven proof dish and arrange the bananas over the pancakes and pour over a little melted butter. Heat through in the oven for 10 minutes.

Wine: Corvo Bianco – vino mafioso! A very special white with a full flavour from Sicily.

Sardine and Spinach Pàté

Serves six

Very quick and easy and needs no cooking. Excellent when late back from work!

> 1 tin sardines in edible oil
> 4 oz chopped frozen spinach
> 4 oz cream cheese
> 1 oz butter
> juice of half a lemon
> Cayenne pepper
> salt and freshly ground black pepper

Firstly prise the sardines out of the tin and drain them, and put them in a blender with all the above ingredients. Turn into a suitable serving dish and decorate with a twist of lemon. Chill until needed and serve with toast or warm bread.

Wine: Muscadet A.C. sur Lie. This has a fuller flavour than ordinary Muscadet.

Smoked Salmon Pâté

Serves eight

A real treat for a dinner party and not too expensive if you can buy smoked salmon bits from your fishmonger.

4 oz smoked salmon
3 oz melted butter
5 fluid oz whipped cream
juice of half a lemon
salt and freshly ground black pepper

Place the salmon bits into an electric blender and gradually pour in the melted butter until smooth. Season and leave to cool. Fold in the whipped cream and keep cool until firm, but serve at room temperature with very thin toast.

Wine: a white Burgundy would be best – Pinot Chardonnay Mâcon or Mâcon-Viré – one of the best villages producing these increasingly popular Mâcons.

Salmon Bonne Femme

Serves four

A wonderful dish I always do when we have caught too many salmon in Scotland or I have kept one in the deep freeze for Christmas.

4 salmon steaks (about 6 oz each)
6 peppercorns
1 slice onion
1 bayleaf
1 wine glass white wine
1 wine glass water
4 oz mushrooms (trimmed, washed sliced)
squeeze lemon juice
½ quantity of quick Hollandaise sauce (page 123)

White Wine Sauce
1 oz butter
½ oz plain flour
7½ fluid oz fish stock
3 tablespoons milk
2 tablespoons cream
salt and pepper

Set oven at 350°F (Mark 4). First cook the salmon steaks in a buttered ovenproof dish with the peppercorns, bayleaf, onions, wine and water, sealed under foil for 15 minutes or until cooked.

Strain the liquid from the fish – there should be about 7½ fluid oz. Make the white wine sauce. Melt the butter in a saucepan. Add the flour, off the heat, then pour on the fish stock. Boil for 2 – 3 minutes then, stirring until thick, add the milk and cream. Adjust the seasoning and simmer for 3 – 4 minutes.

Make the quick Hollandaise sauce. Cook the mushrooms quickly in 1 tablespoon water and squeeze of lemon juice.

Put the salmon steaks on a serving dish, coat with the white wine sauce, scatter over the mushrooms and then pour over the Hollandaise sauce. Glaze under the grill and serve at once.

Wine: Pouilly Fumé de Ladoucette. A great English favourite – and an exceptionally good wine from the Loire Valley's central Vineyards.

He's caught a crab!

Fillets of Sole in Creamy Curried Prawn Sauce

Serves four

I always use lemon sole as it is so much cheaper than Dover sole.

> 2 filletted soles (1¼ lb – 1½ lb each)
> 8 oz shelled prawns
> ½ small onion, finely chopped
> juice of half a lemon
> 1 glass white wine (dry)
> ⅓ teaspoon curry powder or paste (mild)
> ⅓ teaspoon ginger, freshly grated
> salt and pepper
> 4 tablespoons double cream
> 1 oz butter.

Set oven at 350°F (Mark 4). Trim, wash and dry the fillets. Fold them and place in a buttered oven proof dish. Season and squeeze the lemon juice over the fillets with the wine and half a glass of water. Cover with buttered paper and poach for 8 – 10 minutes.

To make the curry cream sauce: Melt the butter and soften the onion with the curry powder for 10 minutes over a medium heat. Toss the prawns with the onions then stir in the flour, draw away from the heat.

Drain the fish juices and pour these into the sauce stirring all the time, return to the heat and let it boil for a few seconds. Stir in the cream and remove from heat. Pour the sauce over the fillets and serve immediately.

Wine: Meursault 1976 – not cheap but worth it. White burgundy has this flavour when it has aged – those with lighter palates should go for a straightforward Mâcon.

Chilli Cod with Red Pepper Rice

Serves six

12 oz rice
2½ lb cod fillet
8 oz peeled prawns
3 oz tomato purée
3 red peppers, seeds removed and chopped
1½ lb fresh tomatoes
or 3 × 400g tin of chopped tomatoes
1 clove garlic
1 teaspoon chilli powder
1 teaspoon Paprika
½ glass red wine
2 oz butter
salt and pepper

Skin the cod fillets and cut up into 2″ cubes. Chop the red peppers into small bits. Skin and remove core from tomatoes.

Sauté half the peppers and all the tomatoes in the butter for about 5 minutes. Season and add chilli and Paprika powder. Pour in the wine, tomato purée and garlic. Cook for 5 minutes and now add the fish and prawns and simmer for 10 minutes. Meanwhile, boil the rice with the rest of the peppers and drain. Run hot water through. Dot with butter and ground turmeric until the rice is golden yellow.

Serve the fish on a bed of rice.

Wine: Tavel Rosé – an outstanding dry Rosé from the Rhone which ages well, turning to the colour of onion skins. Beaujolais A.C.

Seafood Pancakes

Serves six

Everyone loves pancakes and they can be filled with all sorts of goodies – fish is my favourite and you can replace any of these ingredients with crab, lobster, etc. making them as extravagant as you like. ½ pint French pancake batter makes 12 small or 6 large pancakes.

Filling
2 tablespoons chopped parsley
juice of half a lemon
4 rashers of back bacon cut into thin strips
1 small onion very finely chopped
4 oz butter
6 oz prawns
½ lb fresh haddock fillet chopped into 1″ cubes
6 small scallops, chopped into 1″ cubes
1 lb monkfish, chopped into 1″ cubes

½ glass dry white wine
2 oz flour
¼ pint cream
1 teaspoon cornflour
2 egg yolks
Parmesan cheese
2 oz butter
salt and pepper

Set oven at 425°F (Mark 6). Remove bones and skins from the fish and discard. Sauté the onion and bacon in the butter – do not let it colour. After three minutes add the brandy and lemon juice, cook for another 3 minutes and add the parsley. Add the chopped scallops and prawns and sauté for 2 minutes. Stir in the flour and gradually add the wine. When this mixture is bubbling put the fish in, stir once, after 2 minutes pour in the cream and stir again. Try not to break up the fish. Remove after 2 minutes and keep to one side. Divide the bacon mixture between 12 pancakes, roll up tightly and lay in a shallow flameproof dish. Dot with butter and Parmesan. Place in the oven for 10-12 minutes until heated through.

Wine: A.C. Sancerre. The Central Vineyards produce smoky/flinty wines – dry but with a full individual flavour, hence the price.

Fillets of Sole
with Hollandaise Sauce

Serves six

6 double fillets of sole, skinned (approx. weight 4 oz)
1 ½ lb broccoli, thick stem removed
1 quantity quick Hollandaise sauce (page 123)
¼ pint thick cream
2 oz butter
2 oz flour
¼ pint white wine
½ pint milk

Set oven at 400°F (Mark 6). Bash the fillets of sole out under some greaseproof paper with a rolling pin and roll up neatly. Cook in an ovenproof dish in a glass of wine and one of water for about 7 minutes until the fish is firm but cooked. Cook the broccoli in salted boiling water for about 15 minutes or until tender. Drain it and arrange the broccoli on the bottom of an ovenproof dish. When the fish is ready drain the juices and use for the Béchamel sauce.

To make Béchamel sauce, melt the butter and stir in the flour. When this has cooked for a few minutes pour in the fish stock and the milk and bring to the boil and cook for a few minutes. Add the cream and season according to taste. Pour the sauce over the broccoli and lay the fish over this. Lower the oven temperature to 350°F (Mark 4) and keep the fish there for a few minutes while you prepare the quick Hollandaise sauce. Pour the Hollandaise sauce over the fish and serve immediately.

Wine: Here is a good choice of white burgundies: Montagny 1981, Hospices de Beaune, Meursault Charmes 1972.

Halibut Steaks with Tomatoes and Mushrooms and Lemon Butter

Serves four

This is a very simple dish to prepare and keeps in a low heat under foil

> 4 halibut steaks
> 1 glass dry white wine
> butter for frying
> 1 small onion, finely chopped
> ½ lb mushrooms, finely sliced
> 4 tomatoes, skinned and seeds removed
> ½ lemon
> 1 tablespoon chopped parsley
> black pepper and salt

Set oven at 400°F (Mark 6). Wash the steaks and lay in a buttered oven-proof dish. Pour over the glass of wine with another glass of water. Season and cover with foil. Cook in the oven for about 12 minutes, or until cooked. Melt the butter in a saucepan and cook the chopped onion until transparent. Add the mushrooms, and tomatoes quartered. Fry for a few minutes and squeeze in the lemon juice. Add another ounce of butter and then the parsley. Shake everything in the pan.

Drain the juices from the fish into the pan with the vegetables and combine the juices thoroughly. Adjust the seasoning and pour over the fish.

Wine: Sancerre Les Jeannettes 1982.

Fillets of Sole stuffed with Prawns and Fennel

Serves four

4 double fillets of sole, skinned and bashed out.
2 oz fennel finely chopped
6 oz prawns finely chopped
2 fluid oz double cream
few drops lemon juice
1 wine glass white wine
1 tablespoon flour
2 oz butter
salt and pepper

First sauté the fennel in 1 oz of butter over medium heat for 7 minutes. Then stir in the prawns and sauté for another minute and season. Spread this mixture over each fillet and roll up. Lay them in a buttered ovenproof dish and pour over the wine and the lemon juice and season. Poach in the oven for 7 minutes and drain the fish juices into a bowl.

Make the sauce by melting the butter and stirring in the flour gradually pouring in the fish juices. Stir constantly until boiling then simmer for a few minutes whilst you stir in the cream. Pour the sauce over the fish and serve. If you want to keep the fish warm, cover it with buttered paper or foil in a low heat.

Wine: A.C. Chablis or Pouilly Fumé. Generally, the younger the better.

Pheasant with Breadcrumbs and Bacon Topping

Serves six – eight

Pheasant always conjured up memories of endless hours of plucking but this really is worth every minute if you can't get someone else to do it! Freezes very well.

2 pheasants, cooked and sliced into pieces
1 glass white wine
½ pint chicken stock
salt, pepper and nutmeg
4 oz butter
4 oz flour
3 glasses milk
½ pint cream
1 egg yolk
½ lb streaky bacon
8 oz fried breadcrumbs

Set oven at 400°F (Mark 6). Clean and wipe the pheasants and set in a baking dish with the wine and stock and cook for 30 – 40 minutes according to size. Grill the bacon and cut into tiny bits; keep to one side. Strain the liquid from the pheasants and use it to make the sauce. First make a roux with the butter and flour. Gradually stir in the stock and bring to boiling point, when the sauce is quite smooth, add the cream, remove from the heat and beat in the egg yolk with a little of the left over cream. Season and fold in the chopped up pheasant and put into an ovenproof dish. Sprinkle the breadcrumbs and bacon over the top and reheat until bubbling.

Wine: Crozes Hermitage (Red): good red wine from the Northern Rhône – the older the better. Full rich flavour will stand up to a properly prepared gamey pheasant.

Pheasant – not Peasant!

Pheasant with Fennel Cream Sauce

Serves four

The wonderful aroma of fennel combined with the subtle taste of aniseed in the creamy sauce can disguise the oldest of pheasants.

1 pheasant
1 bayleaf
1 sprig parsley
salt and black pepper
½ onion
1 small bulb fennel
2 – 3 level tablespoons flour

2 oz butter
¼ pint white wine
1 tablespoon brandy
2½ fluid oz double cream
¼ lb ham cut into tiny strips
parsley to garnish

Set oven at 350°F (Mark 4). Joint the pheasant and make a stock using the carcass and giblets, parsley, bayleaf and seasoning. This should take about half an hour. Have ¼ pint stock ready for the sauce.

Slice the fennel and onion into round strips and sauté in the butter for a few minutes, and remove. Sauté the pheasant bits coated with flour until golden brown. Stir in sufficient flour to absorb the fat. Blend in the wine and brandy and ½ pint of the stock, add the fennel and onions. Bring to simmering point and transfer to the oven.

Cook for 45 minutes or until tender. Remove the pheasant onto a serving dish. Simmer the sauce and stir in the cream. Pour this over the pheasant, finely chop the parsley and sprinkle with the chopped ham over the top. Heat through for 15 – 20 minutes before serving if it has been made in advance – but omit the parsley and ham until the last minute.

Wine: good red Rhônes come into their own with game. Red Hermitage Jaboulet 1977 – give it plenty of time to breath, this also applies to Châteauneuf du Pape Vauclaire 1980 – try to find ones with more age if you can.

Cold Chicken in Crab Sauce

Serves six

This dish looks so pretty on a buffet table in the summer or an informal party in the garden and can be made the day before if kept in a fridge under clingfilm.

> 3½ lb fresh chicken roasted in foil to keep moist
> 8 oz crab meat (½ red and ½ white meat)
> 1 packet flaked almonds
> 2 teaspoons tomato purée
> 1 teaspoon Worcester sauce
> a few drops of tabasco sauce
> salt and freshly ground black pepper
> 5 fluid oz mayonnaise
> 5 fluid oz whipped cream
> 1 small carton set natural yogurt
> 1 lettuce washed and dried

Set oven at 400°F (Mark 6). Roast the chicken for 45 minutes or until cooked. When it is cool enough cut the chicken up into 1″ cubes and put into a big mixing bowl. Fold in the mayonnaise, yogurt, crab and season. Stir in the sauces and the purée and finally the cream.

Arrange the lettuce leaves on a serving dish and pile on the chicken mixture. Quickly toast the almonds in a tin in the oven for 3 – 4 minutes and when cooled sprinkle over the dish.

Wine: a Pouilly Fuissé or Montagny. A good white Burgundy is unbeatable but tends to cost upwards of £4.50 per bottle.

Cold Chicken in Tuna Fish Sauce

Serves six

Another excellent summer buffet dish and always very popular.

       6 cooked chicken breasts
       1 lb tuna fish
       ¼ pint mayonnaise
       ¼ pint sour cream
       ¼ pint set natural yoghurt
       1 tablespoon lemon juice
       Paprika pepper
       salt and freshly ground black pepper
       parsley to decorate
       lettuce

Arrange the lettuce on the serving dish. In a mixing bowl mash the tuna fish with all the other ingredients. This can of course be done in an electric mixer for a few seconds only.

Pour this over the chicken breasts and decorate with parsley. It keeps well in the fridge for a couple of days, keep under cling film and decorate it just before serving.

Wine: Vinho Verdi – a refreshing young white wine from Portugal, with a hint of a sparkle (pettilant).

Chicken Lasagne

Serves eight

This can be made well in advance and warmed up and is a very economic party dish. Serve with a tossed green salad. It freezes very well.

300 grms green lasagne
1 pint quick tomato sauce (page 122)
1 lb of chopped spinach
3 lb chicken – cooked and finely chopped
nutmeg, salt and pepper
¼ pint single cream
2 glasses white wine
½ pint chicken stock
4 oz butter
4 oz flour
3 oz grated Cheddar or Gruyère

Set oven at 400°F (Mark 6). Use the lasagne as instructed. Melt the butter and toss the chopped chicken and spinach and season well. Bind the mixture with the flour and gradually pour in the wine, stock and the cream until it has boiled. Remove from the heat. Spread half the tomato sauce into the bottom of the dish, put a layer of lasagne over this, then pour over a third of the chicken mixture. Repeat with the lasagne and chicken mixture until the dish is nearly full.

Finish off with the rest of the tomato sauce and sprinkle with grated cheese. Cook for 20 minutes until crisp and bubbly on top.

Wine: Muscadet Sèvre et Maine.

Chicken in Avocado and Bacon Sauce

Serves six

This is such an unusual combination but everybody raves about it and is always trying to find out the recipe.

6 portions of cooked chicken
2 avocado pears, peeled and sliced
¼ pint chicken stock
¼ pint thick cream
2 oz butter
1 small onion
2 teaspoons freshly grated ginger
½ lb bacon grilled until crispy and finely chopped
salt and freshly ground black pepper

Set oven at 400°F (Mark 6). Peel and slice the onions very finely and sauté with the spices in the butter until transparent. Leave on one side. Meanwhile, liquidize the avocados, stock and cream.

Mix in the onions and pour the mixture over the chicken in an ovenproof dish. Sprinkle over the bacon and heat through for 20 minutes.

Wine: Riesling d'Alsace.

Chicken in Honey and Mustard

Serves six

This is a wickedly easy dish and scrummy hot or cold.

> 6 portions of fresh chicken
> 2 desertspoons of butter
> 2 generous tablespoons of mild grain mustard
> 6 tablespoons of runny honey
> season according to taste with salt and pepper

Set oven at 400°F (Mark 6). Mix all the ingredients together and bubble up in a saucepan until the butter has melted. Pour this over the chicken portions and roast in the oven for 30 minutes or until cooked. Baste occasionally until crispy and well coated. Drain any excess oil off and arrange the chicken with the sauce poured over it.

This is best served with a salad in summer or baked potatoes and hot vegetables in the winter.

Wine: Here are two white crisp wines: Muscadet or Bourgogne Aligoté.

Petit Poussin au Fromage Blanc

Serves six

Sadly vodka is seldom used in our cooking but here, with cream cheese and mushrooms, it is delicious.

2 petit poussins
2 oz fromage blanc or skimmed milk soft cheese
2 oz butter
1 tablespoon oil
6 tablespoons vodka
1 bayleaf
1 shallot finely chopped
1 glass sweet sherry
¾ lb mushrooms thinly sliced
¼ pint cream
Paprika, salt and pepper

Dust the petit poussins with the seasoning and divide the cheese between them. Brown the chickens in the oil and butter, add the vodka and light it. Add the shallot and bayleaf. Cover the pan and simmer for ½ hour adding the wine and the mushrooms half way through. Simmer for another half an hour. Put the chickens on a serving dish. Reheat sauce and adjust the seasoning, add the cream and thicken with 1 teaspoon cornflour mixed with a little water, whisking all the time. Pour a little of the sauce over the chickens and serve the rest separately.

Wine: Côtes du Rhône Blanc; Crozes Hermitage 1977. Not well enough known – the Northern Rhône produces very good white wines!

Petit Poussin in Sherry and Tomatoes

Serves four

A lovely light dish, very good for figure conscious guests!

        1 small or ½ a large petit poussin per person
        ¾ glass of medium sweet sherry
        5 fluid oz chicken stock
        1 teaspoon fresh tarragon (½ teaspoon of dried will do)
        4 fresh tomatoes, skinned and seeded and halved
        ½ lb finely sliced mushrooms
        2 teaspoons of cornflour
        4 oz butter

Set oven at 400°F (Mark 6). Clean the poussins and rub with butter and tarragon and seasoning. Roast in the oven for 5 minutes. Remove from the oven and throw in the mushrooms and tomatoes. Return to the oven for 5 minutes. Take the chicken out of the oven and pour over the stock and sherry and finish cooking for 5 – 10 minutes according to size or until juices run clear when pierced with a skewer.

Mix the cornflour with a little water and stir this into the sauce. Boil up for one minute and serve immediately spooned over the poussins.

Wine: you need a medium dry white wine: Vouvray – with age the good vintages become outstanding, or Tavel Rosé – also dry (the best rosés come from the Rhône valley)

Duck with Figs and Honey

Serves four

A deliciously aromatic dinner party dish. Can be cooked in advance and warmed up.

    1 duck (approx. 5 lbs)
    salt and black pepper
    1 oz butter
    1 oz oil
    8 fresh figs or 1 lb dried figs – preferably sun-dried
    4 tablespoons honey
    ½ pint dry white wine
    2 teaspoons ground cinnamon
    2 cloves garlic crushed
    ½ pint stock
    2 teaspoons cornflour in a little water
    parsley to garnish

Set oven at 400°F (Mark 6). Joint the duck into four equal portions. Rub them all over with the cinnamon. Heat the butter and oil and fry duck over a high heat until just browned on both sides. Stir in the garlic and fry for a few minutes. Arrange duck in a shallow casserole dish, with the dried figs and honey, wine and stock and bring to simmering point and transfer to oven for 1 hour or until the duck is tender. If you are using fresh figs, peel them and add after ½ hour. Skim off any fat. Lift out the duck and arrange on a serving dish, keep warm. Stir the cornflour into the sauce to thicken and pour it over the duck. Garnish with parsley.

Wine: good burgundy – but inexpensive; Hautes Côtes de Beaune/Nuits (Henri de Villamont) or a a southern Rhône – Châteauneuf du Pape.

Out for a Duck

Duck with Black Cherry Sauce

Serves four

This dish is even more delicious if you are lucky enough to have wild duck. Cook the duck until the skin is crispy but the meat is slightly pink inside.

4 lb duckling or 4 wild ducks
8 oz tin black cherries
1 small sliced onion
1 tablespoon butter
2 heaped tablespoons redcurrant jelly
1 pint tawny port
¼ pint game or chicken stock
¼ pint fresh or frozen concentrated orange juice
1 bayleaf
salt and pepper
pinch Cayenne pepper
1 teaspoon cornflour

Roast the duck in the oven, basting regularly for about 40 – 50 minutes or when cooked to your liking. Drain the cherries and reserve the juice. Meanwhile simmer the onion in the butter until transparent and add the stock and cherry juice and simmer slowly with all the other ingredients for about 20 minutes (except the cherries).

Remove the bayleaf and thicken the sauce with the cornflour and a little water and stir in the cherries. Keep warm whilst carving the duck and pour half the sauce over. Serve the rest separately in a sauce boat.

Wine: a good burgundy is needed: Corton, Clos de Meix 1979. Or, slightly cheaper, try a Rioja: Berberana Gran Reserva 1970 – one of the better older Spanish wines.

Ginger Lamb and Nutty Rice Pilaf

Serves six

Gorgeous Eastern smells waft through the air as you prepare this dish.
The rice pilaf is full of caramalized fruit and nuts and you can use it
with any spicy dish.

> 2½ lb fillet end of leg of lamb
> 1 tablespoon of oil
> 1 oz butter
> 1 large onion, finely chopped
> 2 cloves garlic, finely chopped
> 1 tablespoon plain flour
> 2 level teaspoons cumin
> 2 level teaspoons ground or fresh ginger
> 2 tablespoons tomato purée
> ¾ pint stock
> salt and pepper
> nutty rice pilaf – (see page 126)

Set oven at 350°F (Mark 4). Cut the meat from the bone and divide into
2 inch squares. Heat the oil in a sauté pan or flame-proof, drop in the
butter and when foaming toss in the meat and brown it quickly.

Remove the meat and add the onions and garlic and cook slowly with
the spices for 5 minutes. Put the meat back in the pan with the flour
then stir in the tomato purée and the stock and bring to the boil.
Transfer the casserole to the oven and cook for about 50 minutes.
Season to taste.

Dish up the meat on a serving dish and spoon the sauce over it. Serve
the dish of rice pilaf with it and a green salad in season.

*Wine: Eastern food and wine are not always the best partners, so either
have a spicy wine like Gewurztraminer d'Alsace or a very light white
wine like Valclair Blanc.*

Lamb Cutlets with Walnut Pâté en Croûte

Serves four

The pâté can be made the day before so that you can put everything together quickly, but let it soften a bit before you use it. This pâté is so delicious why not use it as a starter and seal it with clarified butter, – it will keep for days in the fridge.

1 lb frozen shortcrust pastry
4 large best end lamb cutlets
or 8 small ones, trimmed of all fat
½ lb chicken livers, trimmed of any blemishes
1 small onion, finely chopped
2 tablespoons sherry
salt and freshly ground black pepper and pinch nutmeg
1.8 oz broken walnuts

2 oz butter
2½ fluid oz thick cream
extra butter for frying
1 glass red wine
½ clove garlic, 1 bayleaf
1 tablespoon redcurrant jelly or crabapple jelly
¼ pint good stock
pinch rosemary

Fry the chops in the butter on each side, with the rosemary, and add the red wine and redcurrant jelly and garlic, simmer for 3 minutes. Take out and add stock to the gravy and boil for 10 minutes and keep on one side, removing the garlic and bayleaf. To make the pâté, cook the livers in the butter with the onion and season well, add the walnuts and then stir in the cream and the sherry. Put this in the blender for 30 seconds.

When the chops are stone cold cover with the pâté and wrap up in ovals of shortcrust pastry. Brush with a little beaten egg and decorate if you have any pastry bits left. Cook for 20 minutes in the oven until golden brown. Serve with the gravy. Garnish with parsley.

Wine: Château Peyrabon 1978, Cru Bourgeois. Cru Bourgeois represent very good value. At half the price of classified claret they offer the classic style and can be laid down for ten years or so in good years.

Mutton dressed as Lamb

Stuffed Lamb en Croûte with Mint Hollandaise Sauce

Serves six

This is a very special recipe and will impress everybody. If you can use frozen puff pastry and make the quick blender Hollandaise, then this does not take at all long. Try and persuade your butcher to bone the lamb for you as he will do it very quickly and save a lot of hassle.

> 1 lb packet frozen puff pastry
> 3 lb boned shoulder of lamb
> ½ spanish onion, finely chopped
> 2 oz butter
> 1 lb frozen spinach
> 1 beaten egg
> 1 tablespoon chopped parsley
> 1 teaspoon ground coriander
> grated nutmeg

Set oven at 350°F (Mark 4). Lay meat out flat, skin side down and cut out any excess fat. Take care not to pierce the skin. Cut through the centre of the lamb with a sharp knife to make enough room for the stuffing.

Make the stuffing by cooking the onion in the butter with the nutmeg and coriander. Cook the spinach in a different pan, drain it and add it to the onions. Mix well and spread inside the lamb. Roll out the pastry and wrap it around the meat, seal the edges and brush the pastry with beaten egg and decorate.

Cook in the centre of the oven for 50 – 60 minutes or until as pink as you like your lamb. Serve with Mint Hollandaise sauce (page 123).

Wine: Chateau Ducru Beaucaillou, 2me Cru Classe 1977 (a good chateau in a light year tends to offer the best value). For an unusual alternative, try a red Californian – Robert Monday's Pinot Noir 1977.

Lamb Fillets and Kidneys Provençale

Serves six

This dish is horrendously garlicy, but simply gorgeous and heavily disguises the kidneys for anyone who is not madly keen on them!

2 lb lamb fillet, fat removed
1 lb lambs kidneys, sinews and fat removed
4 – 6 large garlic cloves, crushed
½ lb onions very finely chopped
1 lb fresh tomatoes, skinned and roughly chopped
or 1 lb tinned tomatoes, chopped
1 teaspoon mixed herbs
1 tablespoon fresh chopped parsley
2 glasses red wine
1 dessertspoonful of tomato purée
3 oz butter
½ tablespoon cornflour

Cut up fillet in 1″ slices; cover with a piece of greaseproof paper and bash once or twice with a rolling pin; each piece should now be ½″ thick. Halve the kidneys and sauté in 2 oz butter in a large frying pan. Add the garlic and herbs and when thoroughly browned pour in the wine and cook for 5 minutes. Transfer the meat and juices to a casserole dish. Using the same frying pan melt the remaining 1 oz butter and sauté the onions. When they are transparent, do not brown them, add the chopped tomatoes and tomato purée.

After 2 minutes transfer this to the casserole. Combine with the meat juices. Cook for 35 minutes in the oven. Remove from oven and thicken with a little cornflour.

Wine: Beaujolais Villages, Bourgogne Grand Ordinaire.

Pork and Celery Pie

Serves six

I used to make this as a casserole but I happened to have some leftover pastry and decided to make a pie. It was so good that I have been making it ever since.

2 lb pork fillets
1 head of celery
½ lb onions
3 oz butter
juice of half a lemon
5 fluid oz double cream
15 fluid oz cider
salt and black pepper
finely chopped fresh parsley
13 oz puff pastry
1 beaten egg
2 oz flour
4 oz tin apple sauce

Set oven at 425°F. Cut the meat into cubes, slice the celery and onions and sauté in the butter for 10 minutes, stir in the flour, season, add the parsley and lemon juice, pour in the cider and boil for a minute. Add the cream and keep to one side. Roll out the pastry. Fill a 2 pint pie dish with the filling and cover it. Raise the edges and decorate the pastry. Brush with beaten egg and bake in the oven for 30 minutes or until well risen and golden brown.

Wine: For a change, try a dry cider. The French ones are very good.

Pork en Croûte

Serves six

This is not as difficult as it may seem especially if you cheat and use frozen puff pastry!

1 lb large packet puff pastry
2 fillets of pork weighing about 2 lbs
8 oz cheddar cheese
2 eggs, beaten
1 teaspoon chopped sage
6 rashers of middle back bacon
tabasco
salt and pepper
1 tablespoon English mustard
2 tablespoons chopped parsley
Horseradish sauce ⎫
½ pint single cream ⎭ mixed and served separately
a tiny bit of milk if it is too thick

Set oven at 400°F (Mark 6). Trim the fillets and slice down the middle lengthways. Beat out with a rolling pin under some grease-proof paper. To make the filling, mix ¾ of the beaten eggs, and all the cheese, herbs, mustard and tabasco and season well.

Roll out the pastry into a large rectangle and place on a greased baking tray. Spread one third of the mixture lengthways on the side of the rectangle nearest you. Place the pork over this and repeat again, finish off by covering all the fillet with the cheese spread. Wrap the bacon around the pork and seal up the pastry. Decorate the pastry with spare bits and brush with the beaten egg.

Cook in the centre of the oven for 40 minutes. Serve immediately with the creamy horseradish sauce.

Wine: Mâcon Lugny les Genièvres.

Pork Chops stuffed with Salami and Gruyere in Tomato Sauce

Serves six

Very quick dinner party dish. The tomato sauce can be made the day before, and you can buy pre sliced gruyere and salami, in packets.

> 6 boned pork chops about 1″ thick
> 1 pint quick tomato sauce (half the recipe on page 122)
> 6 thin slices danish salami – remove the skin first
> 6 slices gruyere
> freshly ground black pepper
> 1 glass dry white wine

Set oven at 400°F (Mark 6). Split the length of the chop carefully and as far back as you can. Stuff the chop with the salami and fill the centre of this with half the gruyere.

Lay each chop on an ovenproof dish and pour over the glass of wine and cook for 20 minutes. Drain the juices and mix into the tomato sauce. Lay the rest of the gruyere over each chop and pour over the sauce and reheat until the cheese is bubbling.

Wine: Red Rioja, Chianti Classico.

Mince and Aubergines au Gratin

Serves eight

An inexpensive dish that goes a long way and can always be stretched a little further by adding a few more onions and aubergines.

2 lb beef mince	2¼ oz tomato purée
2 large onions finely sliced	oil for cooking the aubergines
1 clove garlic crushed	3 medium sized aubergines (sliced)
2 oz butter/margarine	¾ lb fresh mushrooms
1 teaspoon mixed herbs	1 tablespoon butter
salt and black pepper	1 glass red wine
1 dessertspoon of cornflour in a little water	4 oz grated Emmanthal or Cheddar

Set oven at 400°F (Mark 6). First stick the aubergines into a bowl and sprinkle them with salt to draw out the bitter liquids, leave them for 30 minutes.

Slice the onions and sauté them in 2 oz of butter or margarine and add the crushed garlic, simmer for 3 minutes and add the mince. Stir occasionally to prevent sticking and when the mince is thoroughly browned pour in the wine, tomato purée and the herbs and cook for a further 20 minutes. Meanwhile sauté the mushrooms in a frying pan in 2 oz butter until soft. Fill the bottom of an ovenproof dish with the mushrooms. Wash the aubergines and squeeze out the juices. Sauté in a little oil and keep stirring to prevent them from sticking to the pan. Now thicken the mince with a tablespoon of cornflour in a little water and bring to the boil. Spoon this over the mushrooms. Lay the aubergines over the mince and finally cover with grated cheese.

Put the dish in the oven for 30 minutes until the cheese has melted and it is hot and bubbling.

Wine: a lightish Claret. Chateau Mylord 1981. The '81 are developing quickly and the abundant 1979 vintage is selling fast. Most petits Chateaux have none left.

Mince and Potato Dauphinoise

Serves eight

Another delicious supper dish. It is inexpensive and freezes well. Even quicker if you have a magimix slicer attachment.

2 lbs potatoes
1 clove garlic
2 oz butter
2½ fluid oz cream
4 tablespoons grated Gruyere cheese
salt, pepper and nutmeg
1 tablespoon olive oil
2 lbs mince
2 tablespoons tomato purée
1 teaspoon mixed herbs
1 teaspoon thyme
1 teaspoon oregano
1 lb onions, finely chopped
1 tin chopped tomatoes
1 lb sliced mushrooms
2 glasses red wine

Set oven at 400°F (Mark 6). Prepare the mince first. Sauté the meat in the oil with the garlic and onions, then the mushrooms for 5 minutes. Then, when well browned, pour in the chopped tomatoes and purée, the herbs and wine and season well. Cook for 20 minutes over a medium heat, cool slightly and transfer to an ovenproof dish. Meanwhile finely peel and slice the potatoes. Scald the cream with garlic. Layer the potatoes over the top of the mince dotting with the butter, the cheese and the seasoning as you go along. Remove the garlic and pour over the cream. Bake until golden brown – about 40 minutes.

Wine: Vauclair red, Cahors – this needs about an hour to breathe.

Ham au gratin

Serves eight

This is ideal for lots of hungry mouths at Christmas. A delicious recipe using up cooked ham, when everybody is fed up with cold ham and turkey.

8 thick slices ham or 16 smaller slices
1 pint quick tomato sauce (page 122)
½ pint Béchamel sauce (page 122)
2 egg yolks
4 oz Emmenthal cheese, grated
4 fluid oz white wine

Set oven at 400°F (Mark 6). First make the Béchamel sauce and tomato sauce. Choose an attractive ovenproof dish and spread half the tomato sauce over the base. Lay the slices of ham on top. Quickly stir in the cream and cheese into the Béchamel, reserving 2 tablespoons of cream to mix with the egg yolks. Add the wine and boil for 1 minute stirring constantly.

Adjust the seasoning and remove from the heat and add the egg yolks mixed with 2 tablespoons cream. Pour this over the ham and cook until bubbling and golden for about 15 – 20 minutes.

Wine: Valpolicella Legoluso, available in magnums.

Paupiettes of Veal

Serves six

Get your butcher to beat out the veal escalopes for you. Do not forget to remove the bits of string before you serve them.

string
1 oz butter
1 or 2 escalopes of veal per person (approximately 3 oz of each)
2 large oranges
salt and pepper
1 tablespoon mixed herbs
8 oz breadcrumbs
½ lb onions, finely chopped
1 glass white wine
2 teaspoons cornflour
1 beaten egg
½ pint chicken stock

Set oven at 400°F (Mark 6). Make the stuffing by mixing the breadcrumbs with the juice and grated rind of 1½ oranges, seasoning, herbs and 1 beaten egg.

Finely chop the onions and cook until transparent in 1 oz butter, then, when the onions are cooked, add them to the stuffing mixture. Fill the middle of each escalope with the orange mixture. Secure each paupiette with a bit of string. Melt a little oil in a frying pan and brown the paupiettes for a few minutes and transfer them to an ovenproof dish greased with butter. Pour over the wine, stock and juice of half an orange. Cook in the oven for 20 minutes.

Drain the juices into a saucepan and add the cornflour dissolved in a little water and stir. Boil until the sauce has thickened. Pour a little over the paupiettes and serve the rest separately in a sauceboat.

Wine: Chablis A.C., Frascati Superiore Candida D.O.C.

Chilli and Paprika Veal Casserole

Serves eight

This is a smooth creamy casserole with a mild bite of chilli and is so easy to make for a large dinner party with long grain rice or new potatoes.

> 2 cloves garlic
> 1 oz margarine
> 2 oz butter
> 2 lb pie veal cut into cubes
> 2 onions, finely chopped
> 2 large sliced red peppers or 3 tins of pimentoes
> 2 rounded tablespoons plain flour
> 1 pint chicken stock
> ½ pint of sour cream
> 1 teaspoon of hot Paprika
> 1 teaspoon chilli
> salt and pepper to taste

Set oven at 400°F (Mark 6). In a casserole dish melt the butter and margarine. Sauté the onions, chilli and Paprika until transparent. Stir in the veal, peppers and crushed garlic and season. Add the flour and stir in the stock. Bring to the boil before transferring it to the oven for 1 hour. Remove it from the oven and stir in the sour cream.

Wine: Sylvaner d'Alsace.

Veal in Mild Curry Sauce with Fresh Mangoes

Serves six

This is a deliciously creamy recipe and rather rich but it makes a delightful summer dish.

> 2 lb veal – cut into bits
> ½ pint chicken stock
> 2 oz butter
> 1 medium onion, finely chopped
> 1 dessertspoon mild curry paste
> 1 glass white wine
> 2 oz flour, 1 desertspoon cornflour
> salt and pepper
> 1 – 2 ripe mangoes (approx 1 lb weight)
> 1 pint double cream

Set oven at 400°F (Mark 6). Fry the onion and veal in the butter for a few minutes and then add the curry paste and cook until soft. Add the flours and stir for a minute then pour in the white wine and the stock. Stir steadily until it boils and season. Transfer the veal onto a serving dish and cook for 40 minutes. Peel and chop the mangoes into 1″ cubes and fold into the veal with the cream and cook for another 15 minutes.
   Serve with boiled rice.

Wine: Riesling d'Alsace or Muscat d'Alsace for a spicier flavour.

Kidneys aux deux Moutardes

Serves four

Very few people seem to like kidneys but cooked like this I have converted many suspicious friends!

    8 lambs kidneys
    2 oz butter
    1 tablespoon oil
    ½ pint cream
    3 desertspoons Dijon mustard
    salt and pepper
    2 glasses dry white wine

Skin the kidneys, cut them lengthways and remove fat and sinews. Heat the butter and oil and brown kidneys, season and sauté for 15 minutes. Whisk the mustard into the cream. When the kidneys are done, keep them warm.

   Pour the wine into the saucepan and boil up, then whisk in the cream vigorously and when it is hot pour over the kidneys and serve on a bed of rice.

Wine: a light red Côtes du Rhône A.C.; Beaujolais villages – or one of the best villages to produce its own appelation – Brouilly. (I think the kidneys are worth the extra).

Fillet of Beef Alsacienne

Serves six

For a very special occasion, an elegant candlelit dinner, this is just the thing.

6 tournedos each weighing 6 – 7 oz
1 lb button mushrooms
2 oz butter
2 oz clarified butter
6 rounds fried bread
1½ glasses white wine
1 teaspoon arrowroot
¼ pint chicken stock (strong)
1 small can pâté de foie (2½ oz)
3 tablespoons double cream
watercress to garnish
salt and freshly ground pepper

Fry the bread and arrange in a serving dish. Keep hot. Sauté the mushrooms in ordinary butter for a few minutes. Put the clarified butter in a frying pan, season steaks, sauté and cook for 4 minutes on each side, according to thickness. When cooked, remove and keep warm. Add the mushrooms to the pan juices and pour in the wine. Boil. Blend in the arrowroot mixed with a tablespoon water and half the stock. Rub the pâté through a nylon strainer, then mix with the remaining stock.

Add to the ingredients in the pan. Reheat slowly, season to taste. Add the cream and spoon over the tournedos.

Wine: Château Lafite 1971 – first growths really are in a world of their own. Château Ducru Beaucaillou 1977. Clos de Vougeot 1964 – over £10 per bottle but Antoinette does describe this recipe as MEGGA!

Fillet Steak with Green Peppercorn Sauce

Serves four

A really spoiling but delicious meal. Something to heat up the evening!

4 × 6 oz fillet steaks
½ teaspoon dried thyme
2 oz butter
4 fluid oz dry white wine
1 teaspoon brandy
4 fluid oz chicken stock
2½ fluid oz double cream
1 teaspoon green peppercorns rinsed in cold water
salt and ground black pepper
4 button mushrooms for garnish (optional)

Season steaks with salt and pepper and dried thyme. Heat butter in frying pan until it is foaming. Fry steaks for 3 – 4 minutes each side depending on their thickness. Place them on a hot serving dish and keep warm. Add mushrooms for the garnish, sauté quickly, put on a dish and keep warm.

Add the chicken stock to juices in the frying pan. Boil rapidly until the amount is reduced by half. Add the wine and brandy, boil rapidly again for a couple of minutes. Stir in the peppercorns and the cream, but do not boil.

Finally drain the juices that have accumulated from the steaks into the sauce, stir in. Pour over the steaks, garnish with a button mushroom and serve immediately.

Wine: Imperial 1975 Red Rioja. Château Dutruch Grand Poujeaux 1977.

Beef Casserole with Red Wine and Prunes

Serves six

A really warming beef casserole, hot and spicy, and the prunes make it sweet and filling.

2 lbs rump of beef cut into cubes
½ lb onions finely sliced
8 – 9 oz dried prunes, stones removed
1 teaspoon each of nutmeg, cinammon, mixed spice
½ pint red wine
a little oil
a little flour
¼ pint of strong stock
cornflour to thicken, if necessary
1 clove garlic – crushed
1 dessertspoon tomato purée

Set oven at 400°F (Mark 6). Toss the meat in seasoned flour and sauté with the onions in a little oil in a large casserole dish. When the meat is well browned, pour over the stock, wine, all the spices, garlic and tomato purée. Throw in the prunes and cover the dish and leave in the centre of the oven for 2 hours. Check half way through that there is enough liquid – if not, top it up with stock.

How about serving some garlic or herb bread with it?

Wine: Côtes du Roussillon. Corbières. These wines from the South of France both need plenty of time to breathe.

Members only, Sir

Petit Pois with Fresh Mint

Serves eight

A very simple way of tarting up frozen peas!

> 2 lb frozen peas
> 1 handful fresh mint
> 2 oz butter

Boil the peas for a few minutes with a sprig of mint. Blend together 1 tablespoon finely chopped mint and the butter. Drain and dot with mint butter.

French Beans with Button Mushrooms

Serves six

> 1 lb French beans
> ½ lb small button mushrooms
> 1 oz butter
> salt and pepper

Top and tail the beans and boil in salted water for 15 minutes. Clean the mushrooms and boil in salted water for 7 minutes.
    Drain them both and toss in butter and season with black pepper.

Carrots glazed with Lemon Butter

Serves four

The sugar caramalises the carrots and cheers up the oldest carrots.

1 lb carrots, peeled, sliced thinly lengthways in 2″ sticks
juice and grated rind of half a lemon
1 oz butter
salt and black pepper
2 tablespoons castor sugar

Boil some salted water and cook the carrots for 8 – 10 minutes, or until just tender. Drain, season and dot over with lemon butter. Sprinkle over the sugar and cook over high heat until glazed and shiny.

For the lemon butter, combine the grated lemon rind, juice and butter in an electric blender or by hand.

Broccoli with Toasted Almonds

Serves six – eight

2 lb broccoli – remove most of the thick stems
1.8 oz flaked almonds
2 oz butter
salt and black pepper

Boil some salted water and cook the broccoli for 20 minutes, or until tender. Drain and dot with butter and season. Keep warm. Quickly brown the flaked almonds on a baking tray – either in the oven or under the grill. Sprinkle them over the broccoli and serve.

Cabbage with Mixed Spices and Cream

Serves four

1 lb cabbage
1 oz butter
3 dessertspoons thick cream
sprinkle grated nutmeg
sprinkle mixed spice
black pepper

Shred the cabbage and cook in salted water for 10 minutes, or until cooked but slightly crunchy. Drain and add the butter, cream and spices.

Courgettes with Dill

Serves four – five

Choose the smallest courgettes you can find; they look so much prettier and I think they taste better too.

1 lb courgettes
dill seed
salt and pepper
1 oz butter

Wash the courgettes. Cut off ends and slice them ½" thick. Boil in salted water for a few minutes or until cooked but just a little crunchy. Drain and sprinkle with dill seed and black pepper. Melt the butter and pour over courgettes.

Chicory and Orange Salad

Serves six

4 chicory
2 juicy oranges
¼ pint French dressing
toasted hazelnuts or walnuts make an interesting variation

Wash and trim the chicory, remove the bottom and peel off the leaves into a salad bowl. Peel and finely slice the oranges, catching the juices if possible. Toss the chicory in the French dressing and serve.

Courgette and Tomato Salad

Serves six

1 lb small courgettes
1 lb ripe tomatoes
handful chopped parsley
¼ pint French dressing

Wash and trim the courgettes and boil for 5 minutes in salted water. Drain and set aside. Skin the tomatoes, remove the core and seeds and chop into 1″ pieces. Scatter these over the courgettes with the parsley and toss in the French dressing. Chill until serving.

French Bean and Egg Salad

Serves six

1 lb French beans
4 eggs, hardboiled
¼ pint French dressing

If using fresh beans trim the ends and wash and cook in boiling salted water until tender. Drain. If you are using frozen beans cook as instructions and drain. Finely slice the eggs over the beans and pour over the dressing. Chill until ready to serve.

Celery, Beetroot and Walnut Salad

Serves six

1 head celery
2 x 5 oz packets cooked skinned beetroots
1 oz packet chopped walnuts
¼ pint French dressing

Wash and trim the celery and dice finely. Chop up the beetroot into the same size and toss all together in the French dressing with the walnuts. Chill until ready to serve.

Pass the Pudding!

Almond and Raspberry Pudding

Serves six

You can make the meringue weeks or days in advance and keep it sealed in a plastic box or tin until you need it. This instant pudding is very popular with children as well as the wrinklies!

> 2 egg whites
> 4 oz castor sugar
> 1 teaspoon almond essence
> 2 oz flaked almonds
> 1½ lbs raspberries (reserve a few for decoration)
> ½ pint whipped cream
> Bakewell paper

Set oven at 250°F. Whip the egg whites until dry and stiff and then gradually beat in the castor sugar until you have a stiff mixture. Then fold in the almond essence and the almonds. Cover the surface of a square of Bakewell paper with this mixture and cook until dry and the paper peels off easily. When it has cooled break it up into spoon size bits and mix this with the cream and fold in the raspberries. Cover with the cream and decorate with the raspberries.

Wine: here you need a good pudding wine – Sauternes, Château Filhot 1974, Château Coutet 1975.

Brandy Snap and Ginger Syllabub

Serves eight

The perfect pudding for the hesitant bachelor. It is just about impossible to go wrong and everyone will go mad about it!

    ½ pint double cream
    3 oz stem ginger
    2 oz icing sugar, sieved
    2 measures of madeira or sweet sherry
    1 packet brandy snaps

Finely chop the stem ginger. Crumble the brandy snaps. Reserve 2 tablespoons for the decoration. Mix the rest together in a large bowl. Whip together the cream and icing sugar until thick and smooth and gradually incorporate the madeira. Do NOT overwhip. Mix the brandy snaps and ginger with the cream mixture and pour into a glass bowl or individual glasses. Decorate with the remaining brandy snaps and ginger.

Wine: perhaps a Tokay, the sweet wine from Hungary would stand up to those flavours. The more 'Puttonos' the sweeter the wine.

Kiwi Yoghurt Fool

This is a delicious bright, light and refreshing pudding ideal to follow a really rich meal with its sharp taste.

For each person:

    1 small carton of kiwi yoghurt
    1 fresh kiwi peeled and finely chopped reserving a slice for the decoration on top
    1 dessertspoon whipped double cream
    grated rind and juice of half a lime

Mix the yoghurt and finely chopped kiwi and the juice in a pretty bowl and add the juice of half a lime for every yoghurt used. Then add one dessertspoon of whipped cream per person.

This can either be served in individual glasses or in a bowl decorated with the sliced kiwi and accompanied with some Langues de Chats.

Wine: Muscat Beaumes de Venise, or perhaps some Perrier-Jouët to clear the palate.

Pineapple and Kirsch Flan

Amazingly quick and easy and the angelica strips makes the pudding look colourful and pretty.

2 lb fresh or tinned pineapple
2 tablespoons Kirsch
2 tablespoons pineapple juice
1.1 oz angelica cut into strips
½ pint whipped cream
1 heaped tablespoon seived icing sugar
1 tablespoon Kirsch
1 large continental flan case

Cut up the pineapple into small bits and soak in the juice and Kirsch for as long as possible. When ready to assemble the pudding, put the flan case on a serving plate and pour over the juices and fill the flan evenly with the pineapple.

Stir the Kirsch and sugar into the cream and spoon over the pineapple. Decorate the cream in zig zag fashion with the angelica and keep in the fridge until ready to serve.

Get drunk – chilled Kirsch!

Blackcurrant Puffs

Serves eight

A superb pudding that can easily be made in one big vol-au-vent if preferred. It will go soggy if kept overnight. You can use whatever soft fruit you have in the garden. Redcurrants, raspberries, strawberries are all delicious.

16 frozen vol-au-vents brushed with a beaten egg
1 lb blackcurrants
½ pint whipped cream
3 oz sieved icing sugar
few drops vanilla essence

Set oven at 450°F (Mark 8) and cook the vol-au-vents for 10 minutes then turn the oven down to 400° until the vol-au-vents are golden brown, and set the vol-au-vents on a cake rack and cool.

Remove their lids and set to one side without breaking them. Clean and remove stalks from blackcurrants and fold 3 oz icing sugar, vanilla essence and 1 lb blackcurrants into the cream. Fill each pastry case with the cream mixture and slant the pastry lids over each one. Sprinkle a little icing sugar over each one and transfer to a serving dish.

Wine: Château d'Yquem 1969. The classic pudding wine – must be experienced. At around £40 per bottle, make sure you've got enough.

Grand Marnier and Strawberry Whips

Serves six

Try and use the best English strawberries as they have lots of flavour. Everybody will be wishing there was a spare one!

6 large wine or sundae glasses
2 lb strawberries
3 dessertspoons Grand Marnier or 3 cl miniature bottle
½ pint whipped double cream
5 fluid oz set natural yoghurt
2 oz sieved icing sugar
1 box of Langues de Chats or similar biscuits

Leave 6 large strawberries for decoration. Cut up the rest and leave for as long as possible in the Grand Marnier. Just before dinner spoon some strawberries into the bottom of each glass about one third of the way up. Then mash roughly or liquidize for a few seconds the rest of the strawberries.

Whip the cream and fold in the icing sugar. Gradually stir the strawberries into the yoghurt and then fold in the cream. Pour this into the glasses, place a strawberry on top and keep very cold until serving.

Liqueurs.

Peach and Maraschino Melba

Serves four

This is another very quick pudding and it is ideal in the summer when you do not want anything too rich.

> 4 glass dishes
> 4 ripe peaches
> 2 oz sieved icing sugar
> ¼ pint double cream
> Maraschino essence (if unobtainable, use almond essence)
> 4 oz flaked almonds
> 3 dessertspoons Kirsch

Pour boiling water into a bowl. Prick the skin of the peaches and place them in the water for a few minutes. Drain off the water and carefully peel the peaches, cut them in half and remove the stones. In the glass dishes, pour 2 tablespoons of Kirsch over the peach halves. Then whip the cream until stiff with the sugar and essence and Kirsch and pour over the peaches.

Quickly toast the almonds on a tray in the oven and when cool sprinkle them over the peaches.

Keep very cold until ready to serve.

Wine: Château d'Arche 1970 (Sauternes). Sauternes are really very good value fine wines. Although very expensive to produce, they cost less than claret due to low demand.

Croûtes aux Abricots

Serves six

As a dessert the croûtes should be a sweet bread; currant bread or milk loaf can be used. Don't let the butter go brown or it will spoil the subtle taste of Kirsch!

> 12 ripe apricots
> 6 oz caster sugar
> 6 slices of bread ½″ thick
> 8 oz clarified unsalted butter
> ¼ pint double cream
> 2 liqueur glasses of Kirsch
> 2 tablespoons sieved icing sugar

Cut the apricots in half and remove stones. Poach them in a syrup of sugar and 6 tablespoons cold water for 6 minutes. Carefully lift them out and keep warm. Turn up the heat and boil the syrup until thick. Pour in 1 glass Kirsch. Put to one side. Trim the crusts of bread and fry them in the butter until golden brown. Keep warm. Whip cream with a tablespoon Kirsch.

To serve, put the 4 apricot halves on each piece of bread and pour over a little syrup and finally the cream, and serve immediately.

Go onto liqueurs.

Apple and Ginger Crumble

Serves six

A filling and warming winter pudding ideal for Sunday or shooting lunches.

> 2 lbs cooking apples
> 4 oz sugar
> 5½ oz butter
> 8 oz flour, sieved
> 2 teaspoons ground ginger
> pinch of bicarbonate of soda
> 2 oz light brown sugar
> 2 oz caster sugar
> 8 oz stem ginger in syrup, finely chopped

Set oven at 350°F (Mark 4). Peel, core and slice the apples and cook them with 4 oz sugar and ½ oz butter and a little of the ginger syrup until them form a purée. Add half the stem ginger.

Rub the remaining butter into the flour, ground ginger, bicarbonate of soda, stir in the sugars and finely chopped ginger. Cover the apples and pat down gently.

Bake for 30 minutes until the top is pale biscuit in colour. Sprinkle with castor sugar and serve with double cream.

Wine: Bual Madeira. These wines are coming back into fashion as a very versatile drink. Dry madeiras can be used as aperitifs – sweet ones for puddings.

Crystallized Fruit Cheesecake

Serves six

This is a really special cheesecake, rather boozey, especially if you can soak the fruit a day in advance.

Biscuit Crust

> 8 oz – 9 oz digestive biscuits, crushed in a polythene bag or blender
> 5 oz butter, 2 oz sugar

Filling

> ¾ lb soft cream cheese
> ½ pint whipped cream
> 2 egg whites, stiffly whipped
> ½ oz gelatine, dissolved in a little water
> 3 tablespoons of Kirsch or Grand Marnier
> 3 oz glacé cherries (reserve 1 oz for decoration)
> 2 oz candied peel
> 1.1 oz angelica (reserve a few strips for decoration)

Use a 8 – 9″ cake tin or a flan ring with greaseproof paper tied around it. Halve the cherries and cut angelica into strips. Soak the fruit in the kirsch for as long as possible in advance.

To make the crust, melt the butter in a pan. Pour the sugar and the butter over the crumbs and mix thoroughly. With the back of the spoon press down the crumbs over the base. If using a flan ring, now is the time to tie the greaseproof paper around the ring. Allow about 2″ above the top of the ring. Leave to cool.

Dissolve the gelatine and let it cool. Blend the cream cheese and gelatine, fold in the fruit, then the whipped cream and, lastly, the egg whites. When the mixture is nearly set, spoon over the biscuit base, decorate the top with a border of halved cherries and little strips of angelica.

Leave to set for a few hours and when ready to serve lift the cheesecake out of the cake tin or remove the greaseproof paper and the flan ring.

Go onto liqueurs.

Strawberry and Rum Pancakes

Serves four

½ pint French pancake mixture (page 126) (replace 3 tablespoons
    milk with 3 of brandy)
Keep aside 8 pancakes and freeze the rest if you do not need them.
1 lb strawberries, fresh or frozen
little caster sugar
1 wine glass dark rum, 1 oz unsalted butter
1 packet of flaked almonds
extra rum or brandy to flambé

Crème Chantille
    ¼ pint double cream, 3 drops vanilla essence
    3 teaspoons sieved icing sugar

Set oven at 400°F (Mark 6). First cook the pancakes then prepare the
strawberries by hulling them and clean them, wipe dry and leave to
soak in the rum and sugar as long as possible. If the strawberries are
frozen, soak them in the rum frozen. When they are nearly defrosted
slice them thinly with a sharp knife.

Fill the pancakes with the strawberries and fold them up and
arrange neatly in a buttered ovenproof dish. Melt the butter and pour
over the pancakes, sprinkle a little caster sugar over them and finally
pour over the strawberry rum mixture. Quickly bake the almonds until
golden brown and keep on one side. Put the pancakes in the oven for
five minutes before serving. Sprinkle with the almonds and carry to a
hot plate where you can light some warmed rum or brandy and flambé
the pancakes. Shake well and serve immediately with Crème Chantille
spooned on top.

For Crème Chantille, gently whisk the cream in a cold bowl until
thick, sprinkle the essence and sugar over it and whisk until firm. Keep
cold in the fridge until ready for use.

*Wine: Beaumes de Venise. Why not be really devillish and try a bottle of
Iced Fraise Eau de Vie.*

Mincemeat Crêpes

Serves six

A definite must at Christmas and makes a welcome change from endless mincepies. Make them as boozey as you like and you can serve them with masses of brandy butter!

> 12 crêpes
> (½ pint french pancake mixture)

Mincemeat Filling

> 1 lb good mincemeat
> 2 oz chopped peel
> 2 oz toasted chopped hazelnuts
> 2 oz glacé cherries
> grated rind ½ lemon and ½ orange
> nutmeg
> 3 tablespoons brandy

> To finish:

> 2 teaspoons cinnamon
> 2 dessertspoons caster sugar
> brandy for flaming

Set oven at 350°F (Mark 4). Mix all the ingredients to the mincemeat. Fill each crêpe with the mixture and arrange on an ovenproof dish, sprinkle with cinnamon and sugar over the top and heat through for 15 minutes.

Heat 2 – 3 tablespoons of brandy in a saucepan and pour over the crêpes and set alight. Serve with a bowl of whipped cream.

Wine: I should just look forward to the port and brandy after this!

Apple and Orange Tart

Serves six

The orange pastry is very unusual and worth the effort. It goes well with the apple purée.

> 5 oz plain flour
> pinch salt
> 3 oz butter or margarine
> 1 egg yolk
> 2 level teaspoons caster sugar
> juice and grated rind of half an orange
>
> *filling:*
> 1½ lb of cooked, puréed apple
> sugar to taste
> juice of half an orange
> 1 orange peeled and finely sliced

Set oven at 400°F (Mark 6). To make the pastry, sieve the flour and salt into a mixing bowl and rub in the diced fat, until it resembles breadcrumbs. Then pour in the orange, sugar and egg beaten together and bind with a round bladed knife. Gather into a ball and knead the dough lightly, cool for ½ hour before using.

Bake the pastry blind in the centre of the oven for 20 minutes or until golden brown and crisp. When it is cold, pour in the apple purée mixture and smooth over. Decorate with a circle of overlapping slices of orange. Serve very cold with lots of whipped cream.

Wine: Forster Ungeheuer Riesling Auslese '76. A great year – and Riesling is the most 'noble' of the German grape varieties.

Cherry Brandy and Cherry Tartlets

Serves six – eight

Everyone loves a Tart, so give them 2 each! If you are feeling very lazy, make one tart for everyone to share!

12 – 16 Tartlets

Pâté Sucrée

8 oz plain flour
5 oz butter or margarine
2 oz caster sugar
2 egg yolks
2 – 3 drops vanilla essence
pinch of salt

Crème Pâtissière

3 egg yolks
2 oz caster sugar
1 egg white
½ pint milk
vanilla essence
1 oz flour, 1 oz cornflour

2½ oz whipped cream
1 lb tinned black cherries and half the juice
1 tablespoon cornflour or arrowroot in a little water
3 cl miniature Cherry Brandy
½ tablespoon redcurrant jelly

Set oven at 400°F (Mark 6). First make the pastry by rubbing together all the ingredients with your finger tips on a floured surface. When you have formed a ball of dough pat it with some extra flour and leave it in the fridge for ½ hour. Now make the Crème Pâtissière by heating the milk. Beat the eggs and the flours and sugar until white and incorporate the milk. Stir over a gentle heat until the custard coats the back of the spoon, then add a few drops of vanilla essence and cool slightly. Beat in the stiffly whipped egg white and leave it until cold under a buttered piece of paper to prevent a skin from forming.

Make the glaze with the juice from the can, the jelly and the thickening agent you choose. Stir them constantly over a medium heat in a small saucepan, until the mixture becomes clear and cooked. Pour in the Cherry Brandy and leave to cool on the side.

Stone the cherries carefully and keep to one side. Roll out the pastry and bake it blind until pale brown and crisp. I suggest 15 minutes for the tartlets and 25 minutes for a single one. Remove from the tins and cool on a wire rack.

Whip the cream and fold it into the Crème Pâtissière. Fill each tart with a little of this mixture, lay the cherries on top and cover generously with the glaze. Keep them all cool before serving.

Wine: 1979 Kreuznacher Narrenkappe Riesling Spätlese. German wine made from late picked grapes which gives it a high natural sugar content.

Charantais Melon stuffed with Blackberries

Serves four

A really refreshing pudding that looks very pretty on a table in the garden in the summer.

2 Charantais melons (approx. weight 1 lb each)
8 oz blackberries – washed and dried
4 dessertspoons orange or tropical fruit juice
Caster sugar, if necessary

Cut off a tiny slice of the top and bottom of the melons so that they sit firmly on their dish. Cut the melons in half and scoop out the middle when you have removed all the pips. Fill the cavity with the blackberries. Pour over the fruit juice and sprinkle over a little caster sugar.

Wine: Muscat Beaumes de Venise

His Lordship's passion – Peaches and Champagne

Peaches in Champagne

Serves six

Ideally simple for the summer, yet worthy of the smartest dinner parties. If you are feeling very extravagant use a bottle of champagne. I suggest Louis Kremer, N.V., or Cadre Noir, Saumur, Brut.

> ½ bottle of champagne or sparkling white wine
> 6 – 7 large ripe peaches

Boil some water and lay the peaches in a bowl. Pour the boiling water over them and split the skins with a sharp knife. Leave for a few minutes, drain away the water and peel off the skins.

Finely slice the peaches into a pretty glass bowl and pour over the champagne. Leave for a few hours to chill and serve with a bowl of chilled whipped cream.

Wine: Definitely finish off the bottle, so go wild and open a few more! Cadre Noir, sparkling Saumur – or go one better – Kremer N.V. Champagne or, of course, Perrier-Jouët.

Strawberry and Mango Compote

Serves four – six

Choose a pretty bowl to serve this refreshing pudding, delicious with meringues or brandy snaps filled with cream or fresh vanilla ice cream and cream.

¾ can frozen concentrated orange juice
1 lb strawberries
3 cl miniature Grand Marnier or good brandy
1 lb ripe fresh mango

Pour the orange juice into the bowl with the brandy, in the summer use fresh strawberries, hull them and leave them whole. In winter use frozen ones let them defrost in the orange juice. Peel the mango and cut into 1″ pieces. Carefully mix together and leave to soak for as long as possible. Use caster sugar if needed.

Wine: Muscat Beaumes de Venise. Ch. Doisy Daëne (Sauternes) 1978.

Lychee and Strawberry Sorbet

Serves six

A much needed refreshing ice in the summer, the two fruits compliment each other so well.

    1 lb can lychees
    1 lb strawberries
    water
    6 oz sugar
    2 egg whites

Drain the lychees. Blend the lychees with the strawberries until smooth. Make up 1 pint with the water and syrup. Dissolve the sugar in the lychee syrup and cook rapidly until you have a thick syrup. Cool.

Add the syrup to the purées and freeze for 2 hours or until mushy, stirring occasionally. Beat the egg whites until they form soft peaks. Fold into the purée and freeze. Beat once after 1 hour, then cover, seal and freeze.

Wine: Muscat Beaumes de Venise.

Cointreau Ice Cream

Serves six – eight

For a special treat this is always everyone's favourite ice cream. Do not be tempted to put more cointreau in or it will crystallize.

> 15 fluid oz single cream
> 3 egg yolks
> 4 oz caster sugar
> 15 fluid oz double or whipping cream
> 3 – 4 tablespoons cointreau or 1 miniature (3 cl)
> grated rind and juice of half an orange

Make a custard by putting the single cream into a saucepan and bring to the boil. Beat the egg yolks and sugar until thick and pale yellow and pour in the hot cream. Strain the mixture into a heavy based saucepan and stir over a gentle heat until it thickens enough to coat the back of a wooden spoon. Do not boil.

Allow to go cold. Stir in cointreau and orange. Beat the cream until it forms soft peaks and fold into the custard. Pour into a freezer container and freeze. Beat the mixture twice at hourly intervals and freeze for a further 2 hours.

Serve with Langues de Chat or similar biscuits flavoured with orange.

Wine: Sounds too good to miss by drinking something else – except Cointreau.

Chocolate and Grand Marnier Ice cream

Serves six

I always have a few ice creams in the freezer for unexpected guests and impromptu dinner parties. It is rich and creamy and is delicious served with orange flavoured biscuits.

2 egg yolks
2 whole eggs
2 oz caster sugar
7 oz orange flavoured chocolate
½ pint single cream
grated ring 1 orange
3 tablespoons Grand Marnier
½ pint double cream

Combine the eggs, egg yolks and sugar in an electric mixer. Break the chocolate into pieces, grate the orange, and put them into a saucepan with the milk. Stir over a low heat until the chocolate has completely dissolved and the milk is hot but not boiling.

With the mixer in action pour the chocolate milk onto the egg mixture and combine thoroughly. Let the mixture cool in the bowl and pour in the Grand Marnier, turn the mixer on briefly and leave the mixture until completely cold.

Whip the cream and fold this into the ice cream. Freeze for 1 hour and then stir thoroughly, repeat this once more after another hour and then seal the container. Do not keep the ice cream for more than a month in the deep freeze.

Winter Menus

Here are two menus which can't fail to impress your chums. I think duck is worth a good Burgundy and for the following menu a good château in a light year tends to offer the best value.

Little mushroom tartlets
Duck with Black Cherry Sauce
Cointreau Ice cream

Wines

Beaujolais A.C. Valclair
Hautes Côtes de Nuits 1978
Henri de Villamont F.B.
Port – late bottled vintage is good value

* * *

Devilled crab and banana pancakes
Fillet of Beef Alsacienne
Croûtes aux abricots

Wines

Soave
Ch. Ducru, Beaucaillou 1974
Liqueurs

Lots of people love games and I have therefore suggested a few light-hearted games to accompany our complete menus.

For dedicated players of silly games Debrett's also publish a book of house-party games entitled *Play it Again, Moriarty*.

The Wooden Spoon Game

This wants to be played with people you all know, best played in the 'lounge' or 'front room'!

Choose one person and ask him to memorise everyone in the room and where they are sitting.

Take the chosen person outside and blindfold them with a tea-towel and hand him two wooden spoons.

Meanwhile, back in the sitting room everybody has moved places, bring the person into the room, twirl them around 3 – 4 times and ask them to identify one of the guests with the wooden spoons only. When he has recognised somebody, he calls out their name and if he is right that person is the next one to be blindfolded, but if he gets it wrong then nobody has to answer and he must carry on trying.

The Wooden Spoon Game

Winter Deb's Dinner

Avocado in puff pastry
Lamb fillets and kidneys provençal
Crystallized fruit cheese cake

Wines

Chablis A.C.
A.C. Brouilly/A.C. Fleurie – light, elegant Beaujolais
Muscat Beaumes de Venise

Now why not try our really fun game to get your dinner party really going!

The Spaghetti Game

A really fun game for everybody, but even numbers are recommended! This is great for 'breaking the ice' at dinner. Find a few strands of spaghetti, or use half cooked spaghetti. One person holds the spaghetti between his teeth and passes it to the girl next to him, biting off a little bit (depending on how keen you are on your neighbour!) as he passes it, this carries on around the table until the spaghetti is finished.

Shooting Lunches

The best part of shooting is the sloe gin, the lunch and thawing out in front of a blazing fire.

It is an ideal opportunity to use up the left-over half stilton, which appeared at Christmas.

My two favourite lunches are:

Cream of carrot and ginger soup
Pheasant with breadcrumbs and bacon topping
Mincemeat crêpes

Wines

A light madiera is always warming at a shoot – and can be mixed with soup
for that extra kick
Crozes Hermitage Red
Port and Brandy

* * *

Cream of lentil and bacon soup
Beef Casserole with red wine and prunes
Apple and ginger crumble

Wines

Madeira
Côtes du Roussillon/Corbières/Cahors
Port and Brandy

New Year's Eve Party

Here is a simple selection of courses for a buffet, as I feel that we over-indulge enough over Christmas and that it is a relief not to be faced with really rich food. It is a good idea to have a good selection of nuts, tangerines and cheeses for those who can't cope with pud!

Chicken liver and mushroom vol-au-vents
Ham au gratin
Ginger syllabub

Wine
Volumes of cheapish dry red – Italian Valpolicella, or Chianti

Now start the year off with an hilarious game.

The Clothes Game

This is rather a wicked game, not at all suitable for disapproving hostesses and rather chilly in Winter.

The game must be played by even numbers and sexes. So if you are ten – first find a pack of cards and divide them into two packs (numbers 1 – 10 in each). Shuffle the girl's pack and give each one a card and do the same for the men.

Now tell them to find their corresponding number. Everybody rushes upstairs and swaps clothes with their partner (how far down you get depends on how well you know your partner!).

This goes on three times until the first person is back in their original clothes.

The Garden Lunch Party

The Badminton Horsetrials Hamper

Hot watercress and lettuce soup
Spicy chicken liver pâté
Tomatoes stuffed with ham, cheese and olives
Fresh french bread
Apple and orange tart

Wines
Alsace Muscat – dry and spicy for the soup and pâté
Lots of light French/Italian wine –
this event is always a blur to me – quantity not quality helps one avoid walking the course.

A Summer Lunch Party in the Garden

A heavenly July afternoon, a long lazy lunch in the shade of an old oak tree – what could be more blissful!
Here is a delicious sit-down lunch, ideal for a weekend houseparty:

Courgette and Egg Salad
(with squidgy fresh French bread)
Crab and asparagus tart
Salads
Strawberry and Mango Compote

Wines
Sauvignon de Bordeaux
Ch. Montalivet (Graves)
Ch. des Coulinats 1975

A Summer Buffet

Avocado and watercress mousse
Cold chicken in tuna fish sauce
Endive and orange salad
Mixed green salad
Courgette and tomato salad
Almond and raspberry pudding

Wines

Muscadet sur Lie (Ch. de la Mouchetière)
Pouilly Fuissé/Montagny
Ch. Coulinats '75/Ch. Filhot '74
(from St. Croix du Mont) (Sauterne)

Three Summer Dinner Party Menus

This is an ideal menu if you are wizzing off to watch the evening tennis at Wimbledon, or perhaps a bit of culture at Regents Park open-air theatre! You can leave everything ready and just heat the salmon through whilst attacking the starter!

Salmon demands a special wine, but I feel that the cheese mousse has too strong a flavour and would not benefit from a special wine.

Blue cheese mousse
Fresh salmon bonne femme
Blackcurrant puffs

Wines
Pouilly Fumé Ladoucette
Saulheimer Heiligenhaus Auslese 1980

* * *

Smoked Salmon Pâté
Chicken in avocado and bacon sauce
(I prefer salads with this)
Peaches in sparkling wine

Wines
Pinot Chardonnay Macon (first two courses)
Sparklers
Cristal Castell Blanch – dryish

* * *

Iced cream of fennel soup
Stuffed lamb en croûte with mint hollandaise sauce
Lychee and strawberry sorbet

Wines
Look for a cru classé claret – '71, '73, '77 – ask for a good St. Emilion, Pomerol, St. Julien, or Margaux, as these tend to mature the fastest. Allow one hour to breathe.
OR for the adventurous – Robert Mondavi's Pinot Noir 1977 from California's Nappa Valley; Muscat Beaumes de Venise

Royal Ascot Hamper

Ascot Egg Mousse
Cold Chicken in Crab Sauce
Selection of Salads
Peach and Maraschino Melba

Wines

Champagne – Krug, Perrier-Jouët Belle Epoque
Vintage Rose (To Match Henrietta's Hat)
Corton Charlemagne (v. fine White Burgundy) '76, '78
Ch. d'Youem

OR

Perrier-Jouëts N.V. Champagne in magnums/jeroboams
throughout the day (and night).

N.B. Remember how expensive champagne is at race-courses
– and the 'fight' to the bar between races.

Parmesan Beefburgers

Serves four

These are very filling and simply melt in your mouth!

1 lb lean beef mince
1 large clove garlic
1 large egg
1 handfull fresh parsley
salt and pepper
flour
2 tablespoons Parmesan cheese
oil
cheese (optional)

In a bowl mix the meat and cheese and seasoning. In a liquidiser or magimix blend the garlic, parsley and egg. Mix this into the mince with a fork. Mould the mixture with your hands into 4 beefburger shapes and dust in the flour. Heat the oil and fry the burgers until tender. Transfer the pan to the grill and sprinkle grated cheese over the burgers and grill until the cheese has melted.

Serve with quick tomato sauce (page 122)

Wine: Valclair Rouge.

Emergency spaghetti – Fish recipe!

Emergency Spaghetti – 2 pints

Serves four

Here are one or two emergency suggestions for dinner.

2 pints quick tomato sauce
1 packet spaghetti or tagliatelle
2 oz butter
Parmesan or Cheddar cheese
1 dessertspoon mixed herbs

Use any of the following:

A	or	**B**
clams, mussels and prawns		bacon, salami
1 tin anchovies		ham or garlic sausage
1 can tuna fish		½ lb finely sliced mushrooms
capers stuffed green olives		1 finely sliced onion
1 large onion, finely sliced		2 cloves garlic crushed
2 cloves garlic crushed		1 – 2 peppers – chopped
Fruits de Mer		*Valpolicella, Bardolino*
Orvieto Doc		*Chianti*

Cook the spaghetti as instructed. Meanwhile sauté the onions for 5 minutes in margarine or butter. Add the garlic.

For Recipe A
Add the olives, capers, chopped anchovies and drained tuna with the tomato sauce. Bubble for 10 – 15 minutes.

For Recipe B
Sauté the onions, peppers, mushrooms and garlic for 5 minutes then add finely chopped meats and add tomato sauce, cook for 10 – 15 minutes.

To serve – pour sauce over spaghetti and sprinkle with grated cheese.

Béchamel Sauce

Approx ½ pint

¼ pint milk
¼ pint cream
nutmeg, salt and pepper
1 oz butter
1 oz flour

In a heavy based pan melt the butter, stir in the flour and cook the roux for 3 – 4 minutes. Blend the milk into the roux followed by the cream and wine or sherry if they are to be used.

Bring to the boil stirring continuously and simmer for 3 minutes. Adjust the seasoning.

Quick Tomato Sauce

Makes 2 pints

1 onion finely chopped
1 oz butter or margarine
1 clove garlic crushed
salt and pepper
1 teaspoon of mixed herbs
1200 gr tinned chopped tomatoes
1 teaspoon tomato purée

Sauté the onion in the butter or margarine for 5 minutes, add the garlic, seasoning and herbs. Pour over the tomatoes and the purée. Stir frequently and cook for 10 minutes.

Quick Hollandaise Sauce

Serves six – eight

4 egg yolks
1 tablespoon water
2 tablespoons lemon juice
6 oz melted butter
seasoning

In an electric blender or magimix process the eggs, water, lemon juice and seasoning. With the machine still on, pour in the foaming melted butter in a steady stream until you have a thick Hollandaise sauce.

If you wish to reheat the sauce add 1 tablespoon water and stir over a very low heat in a small saucepan. Serve immediately.

Mint Hollandaise Sauce

Follow the quick Hollandaise sauce recipe and process 1 large handful fresh mint with the egg yolks.

or you can use 3 tablespoons of mint sauce.

Shortcrust Pastry

5 oz plain flour
pinch salt
3 oz butter or margarine
1 egg yolk
1½ teaspoons caster sugar
3 – 4 teaspoons water

Sift the flour and salt into a wide bowl. Cut up the fat and rub it into the flour with the fingertips until mixture resembles breadcrumbs. Mix the egg yolk, sugar and water together and pour into the pastry mixture. Stir it with a round edged knife until the mixture resembles a dough. When you have a ball of dough turn it onto a floured surface, knead briefly and keep in a cool place for 30 minutes before use.

Savoury Shortcrust Pastry

4 oz plain flour salt and pepper
pinch Cayenne pepper
2 oz shortening
1 oz Parmesan cheese (grated)
1 egg yolk and 1 tablespoon water
1 dessertspoon curry powder

Sift the flour, a pinch of salt and a shake of Cayenne in a wide bowl.

Cut up the fat and rub into the flour with the fingertips until the mixture resembles fine breadcrumbs, blend in the grated cheese and egg yolk and water; distribute evenly and use a little bit more water if necessary to give a stiff dough.

Knead the dough lightly on a floured surface and chill for half an hour.

French Dressing

Approximately ⅓ pint

6 tablespoons oil
2 tablespoons vinegar
1 level teaspoon mustard
1 dessertspoon finely chopped herbs
1 – 2 cloves freshly crushed garlic
salt and black pepper
caster sugar (optional)

Put the mustard, oil and vinegar together in a bowl or screw top jar and whisk or shake all the ingredients together. Chill in the fridge until ready to serve.

Magimix Mayonnaise

2 egg yolks
½ teaspoon Dijon Mustard
2 tablespoons white wine vinegar
½ pint olive oil
seasoning

Process the egg yolks with the mustard and vinegar and seasoning. Steadily pour in the olive oil until you have a thick mayonnaise.

Nutty Rice Pilaf

Serves six

8 oz rice
¾ pint stock
2 oz butter
4 oz brown sugar
1 teaspoon ground ginger

1 teaspoon freshly grated ginger
3 oz sultanas
2 × 1.8 oz packets flaked almonds
2 bananas
juice of 1 lemon

Cook the rice in the stock until all the stock has been absorbed and replace with a little water if the rice is still not cooked. Drain the rice and set aside.

In a frying pan melt the butter and sugar, add the gingers and the sultanas and the flaked almonds. Cook together until caramalised and in a sticky syrup. Just before you are ready to serve, slice up the bananas and add them to the mixture, with the lemon juice.

Cook briefly and mix this with the rice and serve separately.

French Pancake Mixture

Makes 12 small pancakes or 6 big ones.

4 oz plain flour
pinch salt
1 egg

1 egg yolk
½ pint milk
1 tablespoon melted butter

To make the batter, sieve the flour with salt into a magimix, add the egg and egg yolk and blend, pouring the milk in steadily. Melt the butter and pour it into the magimix whilst it is on and leave for 30 minutes.

If making it by hand then stir the egg and flour mixure in a mixing bowl and pour in ½ the milk, then when smooth, the butter and then the remaining milk.

Fry paper thin pancakes in a greased pan and layer them with grease proof paper, or keep them under a clean dish cloth.

Aperitifs

Garveys sherries are from Jerez and are very good value as well. The San Patricio is good and its 'saltiness' prepares the gastric juices for the delights ahead. Their range includes a rich cream, Amontillado and Fino.

Cocktails

Six o'clock strikes! The relief is immense. This is the best time of the day. But beware! New Cocktail Bars and new cocktails must be treated with caution. At home you can avoid the fruit and ensure the alcoholic strength. Stick to the traditional recipes – these are still around because they work. The ingredients complement one another. A Dry Martini, 8 – 16 parts gin to 1 part Dry Vermouth in a chilled glass, is perfection. So are Sours and Highballs. Champagne is of course a welcome sight.

Champagne

Since 1843, The Krug family have remained faithful to their traditional style. They still use oak casks to ferment their wines, and the secret of the blend for their Grande Cuvée has remained within the family for four generations. Krug ages for a minimum of six years – far longer than legally necessary – giving a unique smoothness to this elegant dry champagne.

I love Perrier-Jouët. The excellent flavour comes from an unusually high percentage of white grapes and has good bottle age. For celebrations the range includes Non-Vintage, Vintage and, of course, their very fine Belle Epoque and Belle Epoque Rosé.

Louis Kremer also produces a distinguished House Champagne – and a Rosé around £10.

White Wines

Burgundy produces my favourite dry white wines, Bourdeaux the best sweet wines – but they are not cheap. The Loire produces many whites to suit most tastes and pockets. Italy also has good-value wines; German wines tend to be sweeter.

Chill white wine – but not too cold as this will kill the flavour.

Red Wines

Claret and Burgundy should both be enjoyed, and are too different to compare. There are now sound wines from all over the world made from traditional grape varieties like Cabernet Sauvignon. It's too dangerous to generalise, but any good wine shop assistant will always help.

Almost all wines benefit from breathing – I decant most wines. Only old wines need caution. Room temperature helps bring out the best in a wine.

Fine Wines

After raiding you father's cellar and opening the Lafite '45 – or whatever you pick up first – leave it for the cheese. A mature Cheddar is excellent. Don't smother a fine wine with food in a rich sauce.

Port

Vintage Port is in a world of its own. At the moment the 1960's and 1955's are drinking well. The best 1963's need a little time, and the 1966's will improve, but can be drunk now. The 1970 and 1977 vintages will take years. Warre, Taylor and Graham are names to remember.

Crusted Port and Vintage Crusted Port are cheaper, with full flavour. Late bottled Vintage is inexpensive and popular. Vintage Port will last a month or so once in a stoppered decanter (but never actually lasts the evening).

Madeira is becoming more popular, and some old Soleras are available at remarkably low prices.

Helpful Hints

A good example of a cheaper wine tends to be more enjoyable than a cheaper example of a more expensive wine.

Spain and Italy produce some very fine wine at relatively low cost.

Although some wines will last overnight, I don't recommend it unless specifically breathing (at a recent Tasting, the 1976 Barolo's had been open for 24 hours and were delicious). White wines should be drunk within hours with very few exceptions.

Enjoy yourself. To hell with the hangover. (I'm sorry, I have no cure, although a certain chemist in St. James' Street may help with its old-fashioned remedy.)